Shadows of Empire

Shadows of Empire

The Anglosphere in British Politics

Michael Kenny
and Nick Pearce

polity

The right of Michael Kenny, Nick Pearce to be identified as Author of this Work has been asserted in accordance with the UK Copyright, Designs and Patents Act 1988.

First published in 2018 by Polity Press

Reprinted 2018, 2019

Polity Press
65 Bridge Street
Cambridge CB2 1UR, UK

Polity Press
101 Station Landing
Suite 300
Medford, MA 02155, USA

ISBN-13: 978-1-5095-1660-5
ISBN-13: 978-1-5095-1661-2 (pb)

A catalogue record for this book is available from the British Library.

Typeset in 11 on 13 pt Sabon by Toppan Best-set Premedia Limited
Printed and bound in the UK by CPI Group (UK) Ltd, Croydon

The publisher has used its best endeavours to ensure that the URLs for external websites referred to in this book are correct and active at the time of going to press. However, the publisher has no responsibility for the websites and can make no guarantee that a site will remain live or that the content is or will remain appropriate.

Every effort has been made to trace all copyright holders, but if any have been inadvertently overlooked the publisher will be pleased to include any necessary credits in any subsequent reprint or edition.

For further information on Polity, visit our website: politybooks.com

Contents

Acknowledgements

We would like to thank Duncan Bell, Andrew Gamble, Gavin Kelly, Guy Lodge, Robert Phillipson, Richard Toye, Ben Wellings and Jon Wilson for their astute and informed comments on an earlier draft of this book. It has been much improved by their insights. Toby Salisbury gave the draft a very thorough and careful final check, and we are very grateful to him for his efforts. Any remaining errors and omissions are our responsibility alone.

Our commissioning editor at Polity, George Owers, has provided extremely valuable guidance and support throughout the writing and publication of the book, and we are very grateful to him for his enthusiasm and insight. More generally, we are in the debt of numerous scholars who have made important contributions to the fields of enquiry upon which we touch, and whose work has shaped and informed our own thinking.

Our thanks also go to a number of colleagues at the universities of Bath and Cambridge for their support and friendship during the writing of this book. Nick Pearce would like to thank Pat and John Asher for putting him up – and putting up with him – over the last couple of years, thereby making possible this endeavour. Michael

Kenny would like to thank Ben Wellings and Andrew Mycock, with whom he organised a major conference on this topic hosted at the British Academy in 2017.

Finally, this book is dedicated with love to Rebecca, Hal and Erica; and to Becky, Euan, Orla and Luke.

Bath and Cambridge, September 2017

Introduction

Virtually every visitor to London spends some time in Trafalgar Square, the capital city's most important public space. Laid out in the nineteenth century, it forms an imperial crossroads, where the City of London comes up from The Strand to meet Westminster at the top of Whitehall and where, to the south west, the Mall leads off to Buckingham Palace, passing underneath Admiralty Arch, once the official residence of the First Sea Lord. At its heart stands Nelson's Column surrounded by imperial lions, a monument to Great Britain's iconic admiral whose famous victory during the Napoleonic Wars gives the square its name.

Set into the walls in the north east corner are a group of 1876 Imperial Standards, measures of the inches, feet, yards, perches, poles and chains, that were once used throughout the British Empire. Flanking the square to the east and west are the imposing buildings of what were once two of the most important dominions of the empire: Canada House, where the Canadian High Commission is based, and South Africa House, now the diplomatic home of the Republic of South Africa. A little way out of the square, towards Piccadilly, is New Zealand

House, a fine post-war office tower, while down at the
Aldwych end of The Strand are Australia House, opened
by King George V at the end of the First World War,
and India House, designed by the late imperial architect
Herbert Baker. Sandwiched between them is Bush House,
once the headquarters of the BBC World Service, whose
portico bears the inscription 'To the friendship of English-
Speaking peoples'. It holds two male statues symbolising
Anglo-American partnership, commissioned by its American developers. Bush House was officially opened on 4
July 1925 – to mark American Independence Day.

If there is a symbolic headquarters for 'the Anglosphere',
it is here, in Trafalgar Square and its environs. This is a
term of relatively recent coinage, first used by the science
fiction writer Neal Stephenson in his novel *The Diamond
Age*, published in 1995. But in the last two decades it has
achieved much greater prominence in political discourse
to denote a group of English-speaking nations that share
a number of defining features: liberal market economies,
the common law, parliamentary democracy, and a history
of Protestantism. It is most routinely applied to the United
Kingdom and her former settler dominions Canada, Australia and New Zealand. This grouping has even come to
acquire its own acronym – CANZUK. In many accounts
of the Anglosphere, the net is cast more broadly to embrace
the United States, once also home to settler colonies from
Great Britain and a partner to the CANZUK nations in
the so-called Five Eyes intelligence and security alliance.
Wider still, and often controversially, the Anglosphere has
in recent times been used to embrace a new set of potential
members, including India, Singapore and Hong Kong, as
well as English-speaking countries of Africa and the West
Indies, all of which were formerly part of the British
Empire. Closer to home, the Republic of Ireland is sometimes included as well.

The Anglosphere has an inherently flexible, ambiguous and often elusive reach in geographical terms, and
that is part of its political appeal. But at its core there

sit the countries represented in the imperial geography plotted around Trafalgar Square. In this book we explore the emergence and history of this idea in British politics and show how the Anglosphere, and the family of concepts to which it belongs – including 'Greater Britain', 'the English-speaking peoples', 'Anglo-America' and 'the Old Commonwealth' – have played an integral role in British politics and political discourse since the late nineteenth century. The complex patterns of thinking that have coalesced around these terms, we argue, enabled leading political actors at different points in the twentieth century to craft influential visions of, and ideas about, Britain's role and place in the world. These exerted significant influence over the ways in which politicians envisaged the main dilemmas facing Britain in the years after 1945 and exercised an important influence upon some of the key decisions made in response to them. The fluid and evolving lineage of thinking associated with the Anglosphere has been directed to different political ends at various junctures, but was especially important, we will suggest, in giving sustenance and shape, in recent years, to the Eurosceptic conviction that the UK's future lies outside the European Union (EU) and involves the resumption of alliances based on deep cultural affinities with other English-speaking countries.

The Anglosphere is a concept with a long historical lineage. Its origins lie in the late Victorian era, when historians and politicians debated what held the British Empire together, particularly those 'kith and kin' colonies where 'Anglo-Saxons' had settled, and whether stronger forms of political, economic and military unity were needed to secure the empire against the threats posed by the rise of rival powers, the USA among them. The idea lived on in the early twentieth century through debates in high politics about tariff reform versus free trade and came alive again both in arguments over the future of the British Empire between the world wars and in the soul-searching about Britain's place in the world that accompanied decolonisation, the rise of the 'New Commonwealth', and Britain's entry to the European Economic Community (EEC). Then, as the 'short twentieth century'[1] came to an end after the fall of the Berlin Wall in 1989, the Anglosphere was reinvented once more, becoming a potent way of imagining Britain's future as a global, deregulated and privatised economy outside the EU. In this guise it forms an important part of the story of how Britain came to take the historic decision, in the summer of 2016, to leave the EU.

In this book we offer an account of some of the main political uses to which the idea of the Anglosphere has been put over the last century or more in British politics. We show how notions of an English-speaking international community were integral to some of the most important political projects pursued in the last century, including arguments for imperial federation; Joseph Chamberlain's pursuit of social imperialism; Winston Churchill's attempt to promote British influence in the face of imperial decline; and the coalescence of a powerful current of Eurosceptic opinion which culminated in the campaign for Brexit. We show too how even hardened Anglosphere sceptics, such as Enoch Powell, offered arguments about the national character and provenance of the English which reflected the continuing influence of this pattern of thinking.

Our own study of this theme follows in the footsteps of many historians, political analysts and commentators, and we draw numerous insights from these works. There is a small specialist literature devoted to understanding the intellectual genesis and constitution of Anglosphere ideas in the Victorian era. Duncan Bell, in particular, has provided a rich and sophisticated account of these ideas and supplies an enlightening map of the various schemes of imperial federation to which it gave rise.[2] Other scholars, such as International Relations expert Srdjan Vucetic, have illuminated the racialised character of ideas about an English-speaking civilisation in world politics and observed the intimate relationship between the Anglosphere and nostalgic ideas about empire, a focus that is echoed in the work of various 'post-colonial' critics.[3]

Others have noted the enduring power of the bonds of trust and mutual understanding exhibited in the relationships between some of these countries in a variety of policy spheres, exploring the coordination of intelligence services and military authorities,[4] and highlighted the striking readiness of some Anglosphere countries to respond to American calls for military alliance in recent conflicts, most notably the recent Afghanistan and Iraq wars.[5] One or two studies have explored the enduring and shifting role played by notions of 'Anglo-America' in British politics in the modern period. Andrew Gamble has supplied an immensely suggestive analysis of the power and growing appeal of this form of imagined community to parts of the political establishment in recent decades.[6] How this category relates to other similar, but also distinct, terms such as the Anglosphere is a complex question. Andrew Gamble depicts 'Anglo-America' as a more encompassing point of reference and uses 'Anglosphere' to refer specifically to the countries of the 'Old Commonwealth'.

There is no agreed definition of these terms to fall back upon in order to determine which should be employed to characterise the patterns of thinking about the Anglophone peoples to which we draw attention. Our own preference is to use the Anglosphere as a label to signify arguments which reference – sometimes very loosely and interchangeably – the values, peoples or histories of the core five countries of the UK, Canada, Australia, New Zealand and the USA. But we also analyse the political use of the term for other countries – notably Ireland and India – which represent challenging and important cases of resistance to incorporation into Anglophone topologies. As we shall see, in certain British political discourses, clear and racialised boundaries are drawn between nations and groups considered to be within the Anglosphere and those outside it; in other versions, the boundaries of the concept are kept deliberately ambiguous and fluid, often for particular ideological reasons.

We tend to use 'Anglo-America' to refer more concretely to arguments and appeals that reference these two particular countries in ways that may not include others, and we employ terms such as 'Old Commonwealth' or the dominions to signal references to Australia, Canada and New Zealand in particular (although South Africa also plays an important role in our account in the first part of the book). These semantic issues illustrate the fluid, and often elusive, nature of the terminologies that have been used to evoke these distinct, but also intersecting and overlapping, forms of imagined community.

Gamble and a number of other academic observers have noted the growing density, in recent decades, of links between British politicians and their American, Australian and Canadian counterparts across the political spectrum.[7] The political Anglosphere is an important, but insufficiently explored, dimension of British politics. Its potency is well illustrated by the pivotal role played by the small group of Anglo-American politicians, pundits and media figures who alighted upon the Anglosphere idea in the 1990s, and became influential and passionate advocates of it.[8] We explore some of their activities and ideas in chapters 5 and 6 and point to connections between what often looked like esoteric and marginal endeavours and the growing legitimacy and appeal of Eurosceptic arguments within the British Conservative Party.[9] This, we suggest, forms an important, if overlooked, pre-history to Brexit.

While our own study builds upon many of the insights into this subject within this diverse literature, we make two claims for the distinctiveness of our approach. First, we examine the Anglosphere as a shifting and malleable pattern of political thinking and practice that runs through the heart of British politics from the late Victorian era to the present day, demonstrating how the Anglosphere evokes and gives form to one of the most enduring and influential imaginary horizons in British political life, from the zenith of empire, through decolonisation to the present day. Second, we situate this idea in relation to the different political-economic configurations which have given structure to and, in turn, been shaped by its political uses over the course of its history. We argue that the Anglosphere is not best understood as an idea whose meanings and implications were forever fixed at the point when it was first invented, in the late Victorian period, and is not – or not just – a predictable kind of neo-imperial fantasy that crops up periodically at times of national crisis.

Previous analyses of this tradition have not engaged sufficiently with the specific and changing ways in which the English-speaking community of nations has been imagined and characterised in British politics. The various meanings and implications of these ideas are anchored in the ideological character of the traditions of thinking that have deployed and appropriated this dream. While the Anglosphere and its conceptual cousins are today assumed to be the natural mindscape of conservative politicians and pundits, these are ideas that have at different points in their history been framed in progressive political terms. Towards the end of the twentieth century, however, the Anglosphere did become the imaginative landscape of sections of the political right, and this has had important consequences for debates about the UK's relationship with the European Union. The tendency to explain this emergent pattern of discourse as a symptom of colonial nostalgia, or as the recurrence of an ingrained pattern of neo-imperial fantasy, has resulted in the neglect of the particular role which Anglosphere ideas have played in justifying and making more appealing neo-liberal, Eurosceptic visions of Britain's future.

Our inclination is to view discourses of the Anglosphere as the source of recognisable patterns of thinking and practices that enable political actors to construct ideas about Britain and how it should understand and approach its relations with other parts of the world. In focusing on how different political figures have given meaning and coherence to the stories about the UK that they have told, we are necessarily drawn to placing emphasis upon the circumstances they inhabited and the various pressures they faced. We highlight in particular the impact of long-range developments such as the steady decline of the British Empire and the rise to global pre-eminence of the USA during the middle years of the last century.

Our study also draws attention to the predominantly Unionist, and particularly English, political provenance of many Anglosphere ideas. In the late Victorian period, ideas about Greater Britain were strongly intertwined with beliefs about the unity of Anglo-Saxon Protestant peoples, which largely excluded Irish Catholics and other groups of British subjects. The decline of territorial politics in the UK after the Irish War of Independence rendered these cleavages less potent in British politics. But, in the wake of the end of empire and Britain's entry to the EEC, the growth and development of Scottish nationalism and a new series of conflicts and demands generated by devolution within the UK have sharpened their salience. The contemporary Eurosceptic notion of the Anglosphere garners little support in Scotland and the Republic of Ireland. Its strongest supporters are English conservatives, and it is with them that it is now most commonly associated. We explore some of the historical reasons for why this is the case in the chapters that follow.

The Anglosphere concept is inherently transnational in meaning and scope. It can, and should, be studied in relation to the different national cultures of the countries to which it pertains – in which, it should be noted, the history of the British Empire and the idea of a benign 'Anglo' heritage are highly contested. Our focus in this volume, however, is primarily upon its employment and implications within the British political realm, as we consider the appeal and character of such thinking in this national context above all. This is partly because of constraints of length, but it also reflects the conviction that, while the Anglosphere concept has been construed and understood in similar ways in its constituent countries, to gain purchase upon its particular constitution and meanings, and to grasp the different audiences to which it is – more or less successfully – directed, it is vital to consider its operation within the discursive contexts associated with distinct political cultures and national histories. Our primary focus is upon Britain. And in this context we argue that the Anglosphere is a vital, overlooked part of the complex story that has led up to Brexit.

1

The Origins of the Anglosphere

The early 1870s were a time of premonition and foreboding in Victorian Britain. In continental Europe, Germany had emerged as a powerful new empire under Prussian leadership, crushing its neighbours and establishing its dominance in a succession of mid-century wars. Further east, a reforming tsar was steadily modernising Russia and threatening British power in Asia, while, across the Atlantic, the United States of America had emerged from its bloody civil war as a powerful, economically dynamic and rapidly developing federation.

As storm clouds gathered over the Victorian economy, heralding the onset of a long recession, novelists prophesied alien and threatening worlds. In *The Battle of Dorking* (1871), George Tomkyns Chesney imagined German invasion and British defeat, spawning a genre of futurist war fiction. That same year, the former colonial secretary Edward Bulwer-Lytton published *The Coming Race*, a proto science fiction novel about a subterranean master race called the Vril-ya who drew their power from a mysterious energy and threatened to return to the surface and destroy humanity. Bulwer-Lytton's book, ranging over numerous Victorian scientific and cultural preoccupations and critically satirising feminist and democratic political thought, was a publishing sensation.[1]

Victorian intellectuals were similarly preoccupied. The leading theorist of British imperialism, the Cambridge historian J. R. Seeley, delivered a lengthy lecture in 1871 to the Peace Society in which he surveyed the long centuries of European war and put forward a startling remedy. Incessant conflict in Europe could only be overcome, he argued, by creating institutions of a higher authority, including an executive solely vested with the power to levy force: a federal United States of Europe. The powers of Europe should follow the path staked out by the Americans, who had created a 'gloriously successful' federation. America had found 'a higher political unit for mankind … a name greater than that of State … a virtue beyond patriotism'. 'That union of nations', Seeley argued, 'which here is a wish, a Utopia, a religion, has advanced a great step towards practical reality on the other side of the Atlantic.' Should Europeans emulate the American achievement, federation would 'rise like a majestic temple over the tomb of war'.[2]

Greater Britain

In the history of political ideas, precursors of the concept of the Anglosphere can be located directly in these late Victorian imperialist preoccupations, most notably in the idea of a 'Greater Britain', of which J. R. Seeley was to become the leading proponent in the 1880s. Just as the idea of federation had appealed to Seeley as a means to ending European war, so too it occupied a central place in the imagination of an influential group of politicians, historians and peripatetic intellectuals who gathered around the idea of cementing the unity of Great Britain with the 'white' settler colonies of Canada, Australia, New Zealand and Southern Africa. For these thinkers, the example of the USA showed that federation over great distances was now both possible and desirable. To hold its own in an era of large states, population growth and global interconnectedness, Great Britain needed to draw closer to its settler colonies, whether in imperial political unity, racial solidarity or both: opinion would divide on the practical schemes for imperial federation, but diverse currents of thought would coalesce around the vision of a Greater Britain that would secure the pre-eminence of the British Empire and its future.

Seeley's most famous exposition of this argument was laid out in two series of lectures, entitled *The Expansion of England*. The lectures contain the aphorism that was to become a leitmotif of imperial study, that Britain had acquired an empire in a 'fit of absence of mind'. By this, Seeley meant that the real course of the empire's historical development had not been adequately grasped. In Hegelian fashion, Seeley argued that the secret of English history was to be found not in the domestic politics of her kings and queens, courtiers and ministers but in her expansion, by war and commerce, into a great imperial power. What unified England's history over the centuries that spanned the Elizabethan and late Victorian ages was her struggle, waged successively with the Spanish, the Dutch and the French, for military mastery and commercial supremacy over vast imperial dominions. England had become the dominant 'oceanic power' and the English a 'great homogeneous people, one in blood, language, religion and laws, but dispersed over a boundless space'.[3]

Greater Britain – an 'old utopia' – had come within reach, Seeley argued, because of steam, electricity and the 'abolition of distance by science'. Russia and the USA had already shown that political union over vast areas was possible. Technological and industrial advance enabled England to unite with her settler colonies. These were not possessions, but 'part' of England, populated by millions of Englishmen 'of our own blood'. Greater Britain, he argued, was a 'world Venice, with the sea for streets'.[4]

Seeley's recourse to English racial unity split the British Empire in half, reflected in the structure of his lectures themselves, the latter parts of which dwelt at length on the place of India in the historical narrative he had set out. India's 'enormous native population', he argued, 'has no tie of blood whatever with the population of England' and could not therefore be assimilated to Greater Britain. Its place in the empire was a contingent one. India had lain in 'a state of wild anarchy' when Britain had taken possession of it. It was not a political community or a country with a nationality in any meaningful sense; indeed, it was not *India* at all. That is why its conquest 'cost England no effort and no trouble'. But, in turn, that meant that its place in the empire was instrumental, not intrinsic. Should India develop 'a universal feeling of nationality, at that moment all hope is at an end, as all desire ought to be at an end, of preserving our Empire.'[5]

In making a distinction, common in late Victorian Britain, between the settler colonies, united by race with the mother country, and the countries of the subject populations of empire, Seeley and his contemporaries anticipated the *fin-de-siècle* drawing of a 'global colour line', dividing the white from non-white world.[6] It was a line that was to haunt British policy-makers as they scrambled to acquire territories in Africa and the Middle East and were faced with claims to equality of citizenship from subject populations. It would deepen further as the settler colonies became dominions and then independent states, divided by history, status and power from the rest of the Commonwealth.

But, in the late nineteenth century, the idea of Greater Britain was more than an imperialist ideology of race. It gave expression to powerful currents of growth and integration, culturally and economically, of what historians have called the 'Anglo-world'.

The Anglo-World

The Anglo-world was not a single state, at least not after the American colonies won their independence from Great

Britain in 1783. It was, according to James Belich – the historian whose pioneering work has done most to shape our understanding of it – an English-speaking world that, like the Arab or Iberian worlds, was 'divided and sub-global, yet transnational, inter-continental, and far flung', comprising 'a shifting, varied but interconnected mélange of partners and subjects ... lubricated by shared language and culture' in which people, goods and ideas circulated with relative ease.[7]

As such, the Anglo-world is best thought of as distinct from, but related to, both the wider British Empire and what has been called the 'British world system', the global economic and political system created by the growth and consolidation of the British Empire.[8] It includes the white settler societies of 'Greater Britain' but also the USA, with which the UK had deep economic and ideological ties in the nineteenth century. As the British Empire declined in the twentieth century, this Anglo-world came to form the core of a new 'Anglo-America' – an economic, political, ideological and military constellation through which the USA first assumed, and then exercised, global hegemony (as we shall see, the 'special relationship' between the UK and the USA is a central axis upon which debate about the Anglosphere would come to turn).

The nineteenth century witnessed explosive population growth in the Anglo-world. From 1790 to 1930, the number of English speakers grew sixteenfold, from 12 million to 200 million, far outstripping population growth anywhere else in the world.[9] This demographic surge was underpinned by mass migration from the British Isles to the USA and the settler societies of Canada, Australia, New Zealand and South Africa. In the course of little over a century after the end of the Napoleonic wars, 25 million people migrated from the United Kingdom to these countries and the smaller enclaves of the Empire.[10] The USA was the most popular destination, particularly for Irish migrants, and drew two-thirds of people leaving the British Isles up until the end of the nineteenth century. Australia became another favoured destination after the discovery of gold in the 1850s and 1860, as did New Zealand in the 1880s. Migration to South Africa was smaller in scale, despite its late nineteenth-century mineral and gold booms, while Canada became the primary magnet at the turn of the twentieth century for British migrants, drawn to the rapid economic growth of its prairie towns. Although the USA remained the preferred destination for the Irish migrants, the dominions together took nearly 60 per cent of British emigrants in the years running up to the First World War. These were peak years for mass migration to the 'Old Commonwealth', as it would later become known.[11]

Migration on this scale was made possible by the revolutions in transport and communications that took place in the Victorian age. The growth in power and speed of steamships dramatically reduced the cost, in time and money, of long-distance travel. Merchant fleets were dominated by the British, which carried something like a half of the world's shipping by the end of the nineteenth century. The advent of the railways, beginning in Britain in the 1830s, opened up vast land masses to migration and trade, and these new rail networks also reached their fullest development in the Anglo-world: the top five nations in terms of rail miles per capita in 1875 were the USA, New Zealand, Canada, Australia and Great Britain. Meanwhile, the invention of the telegraph collapsed distances in time and space, as cables laid overland and undersea brought near-instantaneous communication.[12]

The 'Anglo-diaspora', argues Belich, was different to other mass migrant communities. It 'began earlier, was more permanent, and its migrants went to reproductions of their own societies, not someone else's.'[13] Land grants, assisted passage, charitable endeavour and government campaigns all played their part in promoting migration, as did the extremes of famine and deprivation. But, once established, settler societies became enmeshed in complex networks of interaction with the 'mother country'. Money, people, goods and services all flowed back and forth along these networks, leading to the creation of powerful political and cultural ties, with distinctive patterns for Scots, Welsh, Irish and English emigrants.

Economic historians have begun to quantify the new cultural economy of Greater Britain. After 1850, consumerism spread and intensified in the English-speaking world and 'British' tastes began to develop in colonial markets, helping to drive trade flows with the United Kingdom. A sense of shared Britishness – both shifting and complex and predominantly white and exclusionary – engendered trust and reciprocity between 'home' and the settler world, as well as helping to shape consumption preferences. Strong personal ties and attachments increased the consumption of British goods in the settler world. While intra-empire trade was underpinned by a common currency, shared language and preferential agreements, cultural ties generated an economic growth premium within the Anglo-world, cementing a transnational material culture.[14] Hard power – in the form of British naval supremacy and armies of intervention – guaranteed its security.

Imperial Federalism

While these waves of migration, and the economic networks they helped create, grew exponentially in the late Victorian and Edwardian eras, proponents of a Greater Britain had antecedents upon which they could draw. Schemes for the political unity of the colonies of the British Empire circulated throughout the eighteenth and nineteenth centuries. These ranged from proposals that the settler colonies send MPs to the Westminster parliament, to arguments for imperial conferences or councils, to political unity in an imperial federation. Rarely did these ideas advance beyond pamphlets, speeches and private correspondence between politicians, however. Their popularity waxed and waned, depending on circumstances. The

Canadian rebellions of 1837–8 prompted anxious debate about how to reconcile self-government in the colonies (or 'responsible government') with the unity of empire, which returned to the fore as representative government spread to Australasia and free trade legislation removed restrictions on colonial trade. This was to be a fault line in the British state that returned with a vengeance over Irish Home Rule and which lives on in the contemporary debates about the future of the United Kingdom. Yet it failed to generate serious support for colonial representation in the House of Commons or any other substantive measure of federation. Empire federalism was a recurrent theme in Victorian politics, but it never translated into a political project that stood much chance of success.

Only in the late 1860s and early 1870s, when it gathered force around the idea of Greater Britain, would imperial federalism become an identifiable, if diverse, political movement.[15] The Imperial Federation League was the institutional expression of this movement. Founded in 1884, its proponents were the 'most vocal, innovative and ambitious, as well as the best-organized advocates of Greater Britain'.[16] Its goal was 'to secure by federation the permanent unity of the Empire'. At its peak, it numbered over 100 MPs among its members and boasted the future prime minister Lord Rosebery as its longest-serving president. It published a monthly journal and had branches and members throughout Great Britain and the settler colonies. Yet, although it agitated successfully for colonial conferences, the first of which was held in 1887, government ministers rebuffed its federalist ambitions, and it disbanded in acrimony in 1893. The ambiguity and political flexibility of the idea of imperial federation was both a source of strength and a weakness, enabling different currents of opinion to marshal behind a vision of the unity of empire, only to crumble into disunity once practical proposals needed support, particularly when these concerned imperial tariff preference. This was a lesson that would be learnt by future campaigns inspired by federal and 'constructive' imperialist ideals – for tariff reform and increased resources for the Royal Navy.

Anglo-Saxondom: Race and Nationality

Greater Britain theorists also had ideological antecedents in mid-Victorian Anglo-Saxonism – the belief in an Anglo-Saxon race with a unique history and destiny. The foremost Victorian Anglo-Saxonist was the Oxford historian Edward A. Freeman, whose racial accounts of English history lauded the 'Teutonic greatness' of the Anglo-Saxons and attributed England's constitution to 'our forefathers in their old lands of Northern Germany before they made their way into the Isle of Britain', from where, 'transplanted to a new soil, it grew and flourished, and brought forth fruit richer and more lasting than in brought forth in the land of its earlier birth.' Freeman's histories were Whiggish versions of Anglo-Saxon supremacism: 'The continued national life of the people', he argued, 'notwithstanding foreign conquests and internal revolutions, has remained unbroken for fourteen hundred years.'[17]

Freeman was highly influential in shaping racial accounts of Greater Britain and the idea that the USA and Britain's white settler societies formed a 'moral community' of the English-speaking peoples. He rejected imperial federation, which he saw as a contradiction in terms, in favour of a common citizenship of the Anglo-Saxon race.[18] The Liberal politician Charles Dilke, who did most to popularize the term 'Greater Britain' after the account of his journeys in the British Empire of that title was published in 1868, believed in the existence of different national types, which reflected prevailing environmental and social conditions in Canada, the USA and so on, but held that each was founded in a 'Saxondom': 'That which raises us above the provincialism of citizenship of little England is our citizenship of the greater "Saxondom" which includes all that is best and wisest in the world.'[19]

As Duncan Bell notes, in *The Idea of Greater Britain*, late Victorian thinkers such as Dilke would slip between biological and constructivist conceptions of race, on the one hand stressing historical determinants of the evolution of societies, and on the other expounding the virulent 'scientific racist' views that gained ground in the second half of the nineteenth century. Either could be used to justify the violent suppression of non-white native populations. As the history of Victorian imperialism amply documents, the settler societies were murderous ones. Indigenous populations were exterminated and their lands expropriated. But, as Bell notes, 'the presence of xenophobia and the role of racism was also indicated by an act of silencing.' Advocates of Greater Britain often simply didn't register the presence of indigenous people in the settler societies of Canada, New Zealand, Australia or South Africa, and gave little thought to French or Boer settler groups. These lacunae persisted in Anglospheric discourses throughout the twentieth century. Where Dilke and other leading theorists of Greater Britain, such as J. A. Froude, did refer to other 'races', it was often simply to place them in a racial hierarchy and to note that their 'weakness' or 'inferiority' would render them eventually extinct.[20]

Pan-Saxonism

Anglo-Saxonism also inflected views on the relationship between Greater Britain and the USA. Ever since the American colonies had achieved their independence, the USA had held an ambivalent place in the British imperial imagination. It was an object of both awe and fear – a lesson in what might happen if Great Britain neglected her ties with her settler colonies, which might follow America's lead and cut loose from the mother country, but also a source of profound admiration. America had shown how liberty and self-government might be combined in a federation stretching over a vast expanse.[21] It had 'emphatically refused to submit to disintegration', argued Seeley, and had 'proved', in the words of the Canadian imperial federalist George Parkin, 'that immense territorial extent is not incompatible with that representative system of government which had its birth and development in England, and its most notable adaptation in America.'[22]

The USA's economic dynamism was undeniable. Massive capital investment, a surge in technological and infrastructural development, and an urban population boom propelled American economic growth in the Gilded Age. Output quadrupled between 1860 and 1900, led by explosive manufacturing growth in the industrial North East. This was the era in which America unveiled a new model of capitalism to the world – of powerful modern corporations deploying leading-edge technologies and organizing production in proto-Taylorist industrial plants – which laid the ground for the global hegemony it would achieve in the twentieth century.

It was also an era in which the US and British economies were deeply integrated. Capital investment flowed freely from the City of London across the Atlantic to finance expansion and growth. Between 1865 and 1914, over £800 million of British capital was exported to the USA, one-fifth of all its global capital exports.[23] In return, American agriculture fed the British market. Grain, meat and cheese were exported to Britain in huge quantities. In 1890, a quarter of Britain's meat and, by 1900, some 70 per cent of her grain imports came from the USA. John Bull was increasingly being fed by Midwestern farmers.

For Anglo-Saxonists such as Cecil Rhodes, here were grounds for a new Anglo-American Empire:

> The idea gleaming and dancing before one's eyes like a will-of-the-wisp at last frames itself into a plan. Why should we not form a secret society with but one object the furtherance of the British Empire and the bringing of the whole uncivilised world under British rule for the

recovery of the United States, for the making the Anglo-Saxon race but one Empire?[24]

Journalists, historians and social reformers argued in similar vein, proposing that empire federation should embrace America in a 'Pan-Saxon Alliance' of the English and American people. H. G. Wells would later call this a 'great synthesis of the English-speaking peoples', with its 'head and centre' in the 'great urban region developing between Chicago and the Atlantic'.[25]

Rhodes was to pursue his vision with ruthlessness and ferocity in Southern Africa. Others were less convinced. The Oxford historian, journalist and influential liberal critic of empire Goldwin Smith believed that schemes for political union, whether of Great Britain and her settler colonies or a new Anglo-America, were a chimera. The colonies should be granted their independence, not bound together into an unnatural and unworkable federation. Their unity was to be sought, as with the ties between Great Britain and America, in a distinct Anglo-Saxon civilisation, bound together by blood, language, history and culture. National emancipation for the colonies would provide the foundation upon which a new Anglo-Saxon multilateralism could be built, 'a moral federation of the whole English-speaking race throughout the world.'[26]

There was a racial core to Smith's thought which emphasised that political equality in a democratic, self-governing nation was impossible when a territory was inhabited by people of different races who were not socially equal. Writing after the victory of the North in the American civil war, an event in which he rejoiced, Smith asked: 'How can there be real political equality without social fusion? And how can there be social fusion whilst the difference of colour and the physical antipathy remain?'[27] Self-government required a fusion of race and nationality in sovereign states, an argument that was to recur frequently in twentieth-century British political thought, most controversially in the figure of Enoch Powell.

Smith's views found an echo across the Atlantic. The steel magnate Andrew Carnegie waxed rhapsodic about the racial unity of the USA and Great Britain but saw the British Empire, and the possession of its white colonies, as a barrier to Anglo-Saxon alliance. The colonies should be granted independence, paving the way for Canada to unite with the United States, in turn facilitating a transatlantic alliance of North America and Great Britain – a union of the English-speaking peoples that would henceforth exercise world leadership. Such an alliance would be so powerful that it would have no competitors. War would cease. Racial utopia would lead to global peace.[28]

Anglo-America

While Carnegie was dreaming of world peace under Anglo-Saxon tutelage, Great Britain and the USA were groping towards coexistence in the geo-political spaces of the late Victorian imperial order. As ever, Britain's primary concerns were the balance of power in Europe and the protection of India, the jewel in the crown of empire. But it had significant interests in the USA's immediate neighbourhood – in Canada, the Caribbean and South America. For its part, the USA was flexing its hemispheric muscles, increasingly assertive of the Monroe Doctrine that the New World was its bailiwick and out of bounds to European power. Although its elites were still divided between powerful expansionist and isolationist impulses, the USA was beginning to exert an international role in the promotion of its exports and extra-territorial corporate interests. It was at the end of the nineteenth century that John Hay, the US secretary of state, set out the country's new Open Door policy by which it demanded the right to transport and sell its goods in the spheres of influence being carved out by the world's imperial powers in China and other markets.

Relations came to a head between the two powers twice before the turn of the century. The first concerned a border dispute between Britain and Venezuela over which the USA in 1895 demanded powers of arbitration, to which the British government acceded. A potential crisis was averted, but the tacit result was that Britain accepted the legitimacy of the Monroe Doctrine. The status of the USA as a new regional hegemon was then starkly confirmed by the Spanish–American War of 1898, in which it had British support. This short war, in which the USA won a crushing victory, killed off the vestiges of Spanish power in the Caribbean. At the end of the nineteenth century, the USA either annexed or drew into its emerging informal empire a string of Pacific and Caribbean islands: Puerto Rico, Hawaii, Cuba and the Philippines.

The second episode was the Boer War of 1899–1902, which generated considerable hostility towards Britain in the USA. Anti-imperialist sentiment and support for the underdog Boers ran high, provoking a public backlash against the British Empire. Three hundred Americans volunteered to fight alongside the Boers, among them a contingent of Irish-Americans who seized the opportunity offered by the war to take up armed struggle against the British state. Here was a conflict that bore the hallmarks of the same liberation war that had given birth to the American Republic itself, and which could not be readily filtered through the categories of race. Yet, as the Boer War wore on, anti-British sentiment receded. The USA backed the British Empire, reciprocating the support Britain had offered in the war with Spain. Relations between the two countries improved. The 1890s saw a rapprochement established between Great Britain and the USA that would endure into the twentieth century.

The international relations theorist Srdjan Vucetic has attributed this to the propagation of a strong sense of racial identity by Anglo-Saxonists – a discursive construct which shaped the practices and strategies of each state and which would underpin the Anglosphere in the twentieth century.[29] Varieties of Anglo-Saxonism certainly circulated within the intellectual and political elites of both countries in this era. Teddy Roosevelt, hero of the Spanish–American War, who would become the twenty-sixth president of the USA, was strongly influenced by the Teutonic race histories of Edward A. Freeman. He championed the conquest of the American West – a 'great epic feat in the history of our race' – and the settlement of Australia as great events of world history. He read and warmly reviewed Charles Pearson's influential tract *National Life and Character*, which, in a dystopian reversal of Greater Britain boosterism, warned of impending race competition for Europeans from the populous 'black and yellow races'. This warning spoke directly to the fears of American politicians about rising Japanese economic power abroad, as well as Southern segregationists and nativist opponents of Chinese migration at home.

Yet the interests of the USA and Great Britain could not always cohere on the basis of imagined racial kinship. America was becoming more diverse in the 1890s, its population infused with a surge of migration from Southern and Eastern Europe. After the 1898 war with Spain, it had begun to embrace a more expansionist, if not classically imperialist, foreign policy. In 1904 Roosevelt enunciated a corollary to the Monroe Doctrine. Henceforth, he argued, 'in the Western Hemisphere the adherence of the United States to the Monroe Doctrine may force the United States, however reluctantly, in flagrant cases of ... wrongdoing or impotence, to the exercise of an international police power.'[30]

This would lead it to challenge British supremacy on the seas. If the USA was to police the Western hemisphere and secure its new Open Door foreign policy objectives, it would require a stronger navy. Drawing on the influential theories of the naval officer and historian Alfred T. Mahan, Roosevelt consistently advocated the importance of sea power in international relations, and he expanded the capabilities of the US Navy throughout his presidency. This would culminate in the cruise of the Great White Fleet of 1907–9, a worldwide tour of sixteen battleships of the

US Atlantic Fleet that drew massive crowds to witness a breathtaking demonstration of US power and ambition. A little over a decade and a world war later, the US government would dramatically consolidate the build-up of naval power that Roosevelt had started. At the 1921–2 Washington Conference, the United States secured a programme of disarmament of the British, US and Japanese fleets that would fix the ratio of British and American capital ships at parity, ending the British Empire's claims to 'absolute naval dominance'. According to the historian Adam Tooze, 'Never before had an Empire of Britain's stature so explicitly and consciously conceded superiority in such a crucial dimension of global power.'[31]

This divergence in power and interests mirrored the trajectories of the British and American economies after the turn of the twentieth century. Although the City of London remained the 'switchboard' for international business transactions and Britain's massive overseas investments and merchant shipping cemented her place at the centre of the world's financial flows, the USA also developed its own deep capital pools, while its explosive economic growth meant that American farmers and manufacturers could increasingly supply burgeoning domestic markets, as well as the new export opportunities promoted by the Open Door foreign policy.[32] Great Britain would increasingly look to her dominions for her food supply, and her emigrants would follow a similar path. In the Edwardian era, American GDP per capita overtook Great Britain's, and by the time the First World War broke out the USA was the richest and biggest economy in the world. Relations between the two powers would now follow a new dynamic.

Imperial Politics: Joseph Chamberlain and Tariff Reform

The career of one politician – Joseph Chamberlain – symbolises more than any other the challenges and choices

Great Britain faced in this era. A Birmingham industrialist who rose to prominence as a pioneering municipal reformer and champion of education in his home city, Chamberlain was a radical liberal who broke with his party over Home Rule for Ireland and became a Unionist colonial secretary in the Salisbury government elected in 1895. He had long been attracted to imperialist thinking and is said to have sent his son Austen to study at Cambridge University because J. R. Seeley held a chair there.[33] Chamberlain was greatly influenced by the publication in 1883 of Seeley's *Expansion of England*, and he refracted significant events of that period – the death of General Gordon in Khartoum, and Bismarck's annexation of the Cameroons – through its imperialist lenses. He became deeply preoccupied by the fate of the British Empire.

Chamberlain also absorbed Seeley's federalism and the latter's admiration for the USA, seeing the answer to Irish nationalist demands in significant devolution of local government to Ireland or, more expansively, in a federal system of 'Home Rule all-round', with an imperial legislature at Westminster. In Chamberlain's political thought, federation was the key to solving both the internal and the external pressures on the United Kingdom – the means by which it would remain united and closely tied to its settler colonies. But there was a racial element too: in opposing Gladstone's plans for Irish Home Rule, Chamberlain evoked the spectre of an island divided into 'two nations, two races and two religions'. He would not countenance coercion against Ulster's Protestant community, yet would readily do so against Ireland's majority Catholic population. In the end, Unionist deference to the unitary constitution prevailed over a federal solution. Chamberlain would prefer alliance with 'English gentlemen' in the Tory Party to one with Irish nationalists.

Imperial federation would continue 'to haunt his mind and dog his steps for the remainder of his life', however.[34] In the late 1880s, he took up the post of chief commissioner in the USA to adjudicate a dispute over fishing rights in North American waters. While in Canada, he would extol the virtues of its federal constitution, arguing that it might yet become a 'lamp lighting our path to the federation of the British Empire'. In the run-up to the 1895 general election, after which he became colonial secretary, he would increasingly fuse the themes of social reform and imperialist unity, stressing that his unionism meant a commitment both to an undivided empire and to the welfare and union of all the social classes of the community. This was to become the basis of his later campaign for tariff reform. It also established a template for Eurosceptics in the twenty-first century: the powerful yoking together of geo-political ambitions with promissory notes of social reform for the working classes.

As colonial secretary, Chamberlain energetically promoted public investment and loan schemes for the development of Britain's colonies, particularly to finance infrastructural development in newly acquired African colonies. He increasingly brought the economic management of the empire into the state's orbit rather than leaving it to private companies – presaging a more self-consciously activist role for the imperial government. This was to find its fullest expression in his proposals for tariff reform. Already, by the 1880s and 1890s, Canada and a number of individual Australian colonies (Australia was to become a federation in 1901) had introduced tariff protections, which also fell on British exports. The settler colonies appeared to be developing their own national economic and political agendas, which troubled imperial unionists. Chamberlain began to advocate for an imperial *Zollverein*, in which the British Empire would become a preferential trade area, surrounded by high tariff walls. These tariffs would help pay for the defence of the empire, obviating the need for direct imperial taxation.

Having failed to persuade the cabinet to back his proposal, Chamberlain resigned from Balfour's administration in 1903 to prosecute his campaign in the country at large. Launching it in Birmingham, he argued that his scheme for imperial preference would not apply to Indian or any other 'native fellow subjects' but only to 'our own kinsfolk' – that 'white population that constitutes the majority in all the great self-governing Colonies of the Empire.' This population was growing through emigration and the economic development of newly settled territories. When critics pointed out that free trade with other nations exceeded imperial trade, tariff reformers replied that colonial trade was growing faster and was worth more to Great Britain – an argument that would be echoed a century or so later by Eurosceptic advocates of trade with the Anglosphere against the European Union.

The campaign for tariff reform ultimately foundered on the rocks of free trade, commitment to which dominated Great Britain's political economy, and also on working-class hostility. The commercial, financial and shipping interests centred on the City of London all opposed tariff reform, as did the cotton, coal and shipbuilding businesses. Working-class support was readily neutered by the fact that, since foodstuffs constituted the bulk of imports from the settler colonies, tariff reform would simply put up the price of food on the kitchen table. Free traders contrasted their 'big loaf' of bread with the 'little loaf' working families would get under imperial preference. Chamberlain's cross-class political appeal to imperialism abroad and radicalism at home failed him at this point. At the start of his campaign, he held out the promise of using tariff revenues to pay for new state pensions, but somehow, 'during the summer of 1903, Chamberlain let this grand design slip between his fingers.' Instead, he promised compensatory abolition in duties on sugar and tea so as to balance the working class household budget. 'Having promised to produce social reform like a rabbit out of his fiscal hat, Chamberlain was left with an empty hat.'[35]

Milner's Kindergarten and the Round Table Movement

Chamberlain's belief in the importance of imperial unity had been fortified by the experience of the Second Boer War – 'Joe's War'. A mighty empire had taken nearly four years to subdue a small force of guerrillas. It had been a profound shock, stimulating calls for social reform to improve the well-being and physical strength of British soldiers. But it had also nurtured popular imperialist sentiment and strong fellow feelings towards 'kith and kin' compatriots from the settler colonies, some 50,000 of whom had fought alongside British Army troops. In the midst of the war, at the 1900 'Khaki' election, the Conservatives had been returned to office and, a few years later, Chamberlain launched his tariff reform campaign. Imperial preference, it has been said, was 'born on the veld'.[36]

Edwardian South Africa was also to prove the nursery of a new generation of imperial federalists, whose thinking formed a bridge between late Victorian imperialism and the era when the British Empire came to an end after the Second World War. This was the group of young Oxford graduates brought together by Chamberlain's ally and commissioner to South Africa, Alfred Milner. 'Milner's Kindergarten', as his protégés became known, was recruited to serve Milner, and then his successor Lord Selborne, in the administration of the defeated Afrikaner republics. They were a tightly knit group, among whose number were Lionel Curtis, a writer, pamphleteer and later fellow at All Souls College, Oxford; the MP and future colonial secretary Leo Amery (perhaps best known for shouting 'Speak for England, Arthur', across the floor of the House of Commons to the Labour MP Arthur Greenwood during a debate on the invasion of Poland at the beginning of the Second World War); Philip Kerr, the future Lord Lothian, who later served as Lloyd George's private secretary, under-secretary of state to India and Britain's ambassador to Washington; and a clutch of future governor generals, city businessmen and influential journalists (at the eclectic fringes of the kindergarten were also to be found the imperial architect Herbert Baker and the novelist John Buchan).

This group, with Curtis holding the pen, drafted the Selborne Memorandum of 1907, which laid out the case for the unification of South Africa in a new federation. Self-government had been promised in the Treaty of Vereeniging that ended the Boer War, but the questions of how power would be shared, and to whom the franchise would extend, had been deferred. The Selborne Memorandum argued that unification was the only means by which the economic and political divisions within the country could be solved and the full freedoms of self-government enjoyed. In the background was a conviction that Britain's future interest would be secured by a rising British settler population, despite the fact that unification would in the short term hand political supremacy to the Boers. But the memorandum was ultimately directed at the white population, British and Boer, as a whole: without unity, it argued, the 'native question' and the political and civil rights of black African and Indian populations could not be addressed.

At this time, the population of South Africa was two-thirds black-African, but, when the new Union of South Africa came into being in 1910, these communities, and their Indian counterparts, were excluded from the franchise in every state apart from the Cape, where a property qualification and literacy test ensured that the suffrage, while not based on colour, did not extend to the bulk of the native population. Similarly, only whites were allowed to stand in elections to the national parliament. Despite having been highly critical of the racial policies of the Boer republics, the British government thus consented to their demands for white-only democracy. The foundation stones of apartheid had been laid.

The drawing of a colour line as a precondition of political unity in South Africa was bitterly resented by the Indian and African communities, who brought their case to Westminster – in delegations led by Gandhi and the liberal Cape politician W. R. Schreiner – only to be rebuffed by British politicians. Despite vocal support from some Labour and Liberal MPs, the legislation creating the new Union of South Africa passed without amendment. The British government gave precedence to dominion self-government and the need for political settlement over the racial equality of the subjects of empire. Gandhi returned home, disillusioned with 'imperial brotherhood' and greatly radicalised in political terms.

Yet, for Milner's Kindergarten, the creation of a unified South African state within the British Empire was an historic achievement upon which a wider imperial unity could be built. On leaving his post in South Africa in 1905, Milner gave a farewell speech to the citizens of Johannesburg in which he called upon his listeners to remain faithful to the 'great ideal of Imperial Unity', a 'permanent organic union', which he believed was 'one of the noblest conceptions which has ever dawned on the political imagination of mankind.'[37] His kindergarten took up the challenge. In South Africa they had drawn up a memorandum to crystallise the problem of political division and to define the solution and had created 'closer union' societies and a house journal, *The State*, to propagate their ideas. Now they proposed to do the same for imperial unity and founded the Round Table movement as the instrument of their ambitions. Lionel Curtis was employed to organise a network of Round Table societies in the dominions and to work on drafting a new memorandum, while Kerr would edit a *Round Table* journal. The aim of the Round Table movement was the creation of 'an Imperial government constitutionally responsible to all the electors of the Empire, and with power to act directly on the individual citizens'.[38]

The first fruit of the Round Table movement was the 'Green memorandum' drafted by Curtis and published in 1910. It argued that Greater Britain must 'federate or disintegrate'. Like imperial federalists before him, Curtis argued that nations were engaged in a struggle for survival that could be won only through common investment in defence and security, particularly sea power. Britain's empire was on the wane, straining under the weight of its obligations and losing ground to its competitors. It was particularly vulnerable to the expansion of the German Navy. Curtis's remedy was an imperial government that would be responsible for foreign and security policy, answerable to a bicameral parliament modelled on the US Congress and financed by existing national governments. Wisely, perhaps, he proposed to leave control of tariffs with the dominions.

Like its Victorian precursors, however, Curtis's scheme was criticised as pessimistic, precipitate and impractical. The dominions, it was argued, were not ready for federation, and the Westminster parliament would not concede sovereignty to a higher imperial body. The exclusion of India and Britain's dependencies from the scheme of federation also troubled and divided his readers, stimulating the Round Table to develop new ideas for the governance of India. But Curtis soldiered on determinedly. He travelled extensively in the dominions, proselytising to local Round Table groups and corresponding ceaselessly with a wide Anglophone network. In Great Britain, supporters of the Round Table would meet regularly for 'moots' at the Piccadilly offices of the journal and for social weekends at the country houses of wealthy supporters. Meanwhile, Curtis got to work drafting new arguments for a British Commonwealth, as he came to call his proposed imperial polity. This he would eventually publish in 1916 as *The Problem of the Commonwealth*.

The outbreak of the First World War scattered and distracted the Round Table group, a number of whom assumed central roles in the war effort: Kerr became Lloyd George's private secretary, Milner played a leading role in the war cabinet, and Leo Amery served as an intelligence officer before joining the government as a junior minister.

Each would retain fidelity to the ideal of imperial federation, and the inclusion of the dominions in the imperial war cabinet, and subsequently at the peace negotiations at Versailles, bears tribute to their influence. Yet events would render their dreams of imperial federation unrealisable. Although the war brought a surge of patriotic loyalty and troops to the mother country from the settler dominions, the bloody sacrifice of ANZAC troops at the Gallipoli landings and of the Canadian Corps at the Battle of Vimy Ridge would mark a new stage in the development of their national identities.[39] The mobilisation of over a million soldiers, and the massive economic contribution to the war effort made by the settler dominions, would serve ultimately as a proxy 'war of independence' for these countries.[40]

From Empire to Commonwealth

At the Paris peace negotiations, the dominions used their separate representation within the British delegation to prosecute their own economic and political goals. The Australians, led by the Nationalist prime minister Billy Hughes, fought especially hard, not only to secure war reparations from Germany but to defeat Japanese efforts to insert a race equality clause in the preamble to the Covenant founding the League of Nations. Australia, in common with the other settler dominions, sought to protect the 'white walls' it had erected at the turn of the century – immigration laws that restricted non-white immigration.

In doing so, Australia aimed to preserve the settlement reached at the Colonial Conference held in 1897 to mark Queen Victoria's Diamond Jubilee, at which Joseph Chamberlain had agreed to a compromise between the imperial principle of the equal treatment of all British subjects and the right of the self-governing colonies to implement their own immigration laws. Resisting race-based discrimination, Chamberlain had proposed the use of literacy and character tests to select immigrants. But using qualifications of this kind effectively ensured the racial exclusion of non-whites, particularly Asians. 'Chamberlain', wrote Marilyn Lake and Henry Reynolds, 'thus helped dismantle that which he sought to uphold: the traditions of the Empire and the special status of the British subject. Paradoxically, the implementation of a literacy test framed to avoid all reference to race helped consolidate the new binary divide between the 'white' and 'not-white' races.'[41]

Racial exclusion intensified after the First World War, as Canada and New Zealand enacted further measures to tighten immigration control against non-white migrants. By now the elastic of imperial citizenship – of equality between the subjects of the king throughout the empire – was being stretched to breaking point. Half of the 3 million troops mobilised in the empire had come from India, yet it was still denied self-governing status, and Indians faced civil and political discrimination in the 'white dominions'. The massacre at Amritsar in 1919 would only serve further to inflame nationalist anger. At the Imperial Conferences of 1921 and 1923, Australia, Canada and New Zealand were prevailed upon to withdraw their discriminatory legislation against Indian subjects (South Africa was isolated in its refusal to do so). Yet the tensions inherent in trying to reconcile imperial citizenship with 'white' immigration systems and dominion self-government would be too much to contain. After the Second World War they would be forced out into the open.

The trajectory towards national self-determination for the dominions was also now clear. In 1926, the seventh Imperial Conference issued the Balfour Declaration, defining the status of the dominions as 'autonomous Communities within the British Empire, equal in status, in no way subordinate one to another in any aspect of their domestic or external affairs, though united by a common allegiance to the Crown, and freely associated as members of the British Commonwealth of Nations'. This carefully crafted formula would be codified in the 1931 Statute

of Westminster, which established the legislative independence of the dominions, including the new Irish Free State.
The nomenclature of Commonwealth belonged to Curtis
and the Round Table movement, but the reality was a
highly attenuated version of the imperial unity to which
they had once aspired. Like the American colonies before
them, the settler dominions would now become nations.

Paradoxically, just as the dominions cemented their
independence, the cause of tariff reform enjoyed a brief
renaissance. In the 1930s, economic depression, the collapse of the gold standard and the outbreak of competitive
protectionism strengthened the political case for imperial
preference. When Britain came off the gold standard in
1931, the dominions devalued with it, effectively creating
a managed sterling area. At the Ottawa Imperial Conference of 1932, Neville Chamberlain, son of Joseph, helped
negotiate a network of interlocking agreements by which
empire countries agreed to give each other's products preferential tariff treatment. Britain got comparatively little
out of the agreements, but the conference consolidated a
system of imperial preference. Between 1929 and 1938,
the volume of British imports from Australia and Canada
more than doubled, while those from Argentina were
almost cut in half. Cheap money and lower food and raw
material prices from Commonwealth imports drove Britain's economic recovery. By 1939, 'Greater Britain was at
its peak economically and, possibly, culturally.'[42]

Lineages of Greater Britain

The Ottawa conference reinforced the splits in the National
Government, as tariff reform had divided political parties
and governments since the turn of the century. Free traders
resigned from office. But although imperial preference
strengthened the ties of trade within the empire, it did not
fundamentally recast Britain's political economy: empire
goods still accounted for only 40 per cent of her imports

in the late 1930s. Moreover, it would take another world war and the election of a Labour government for the social dividends long promised by constructive imperialists to be paid down in the creation of a comprehensive welfare state.

What then endured from this heritage of interlocking thought and practice that constituted Greater Britain, and its Atlanticist cousin Anglo-America, as another global conflict loomed over the horizon? Imperial federalists had failed to create an institutional union to match the imagined community of Greater Britain, but the economic, cultural and political ties between the settler dominions and the mother country were nonetheless real and strong. It is these ties that allow James Belich to argue that 'Greater Britain was a relatively short-lived entity, with a life span of less than a century, say 1880s to 1960s. But it was big and powerful in its day, a virtual United States, which historians of the period can no longer ignore, nor dismiss as a failed idea.'[43]

To illustrate his point, when the Second World War broke out, the dominions once again mobilised troops in their millions and put their economies at the service of Britain's war effort. Yet the huge burden of fighting the war, and the great strategic defeats it suffered between 1940 and 1942, put paid to the idea that the mother country could ultimately guarantee the security of the settler dominions. Canada, Australia and New Zealand would increasingly turn to the USA as the guarantor of their security.[44] For its part, Ireland would remain neutral and, before long, become a republic. India would also achieve independence within short order. The racial and national foundations that had both undergirded and undermined ideas of Greater Britain would crumble in the post-war period.

Yet war also brought federalist ideas back into vogue. Lord Lothian, as Phillip Kerr had become, argued in 1935 that war could be averted and human flourishing achieved only if 'enough citizens of national states, while retaining their full autonomy in national affairs, are willing to form themselves into a world nation for common purposes.'[45] Imperial federation had thus morphed into international federation. With William Beveridge, Lionel Robbins, Barbara Wootton and others, Lothian helped set up a Federal Union in 1938. It had branches all over the UK and thousands of members. In the early 1940s, by which time Lothian had died of overwork as Britain's ambassador to the USA, his friend and Round Table collaborator Lionel Curtis penned *World War, its Cause and Cure*, arguing that federal integration was the only means by which war could be prevented.[46] Just as John Seeley had done seventy years earlier, Curtis urged the nations of Western Europe to integrate and join Greater Britain in a new union for mutual defence and security. If the USA were to join such a union, he argued, echoing Andrew Carnegie, the era of world wars would be 'finally over'.[47]

This federalist tradition would remain a largely subterranean one in British political thought, but it was powerfully renewed by European federalists after the Second World War. The heirs of the Victorian idea of imperial federalism would turn in two directions: those who prioritised peace and security would make the case for European unity and greater international cooperation in the United Nations, while those who inherited the Anglo-Saxonist 'kith and kin' tradition would fall back towards unitary sovereignty and the nation-state, seeking allies and economic ties, but not political union, in the Anglosphere. The figure of Winston Churchill would loom large over these debates and straddle both of these perspectives, as we shall now see.

2

After Empire: The Rise of the 'English-Speaking Peoples'

The ensemble of ideas about Greater Britain which began to coalesce in the late nineteenth century percolated into the British state, the main political parties and the wider culture. But these schemes and visions met with growing scepticism in the early part of the next century. They were challenged, in particular, by the profound political instability and economic dislocation of the 1930s and the growing spectre of military conflict in Europe. Anxieties about Britain's place in the world rose as free trade was increasingly under threat, the 'white dominions' demanded greater autonomy, and it became increasingly apparent that the days of empire might well be numbered. The USA was now a major power in its own right and had steadily overtaken Britain as an economic power.

This chapter explores some of the strains and tensions generated by these developments and looks in particular at Winston Churchill's supple and evolving thinking about the different transnational allegiances which Britain should hold on to in order to maintain its power and influence – Anglo-America, the empire, the Commonwealth and Europe. It also explores his unique, and rather ambivalent, contribution to post-war thinking about Britain's geo-political position and future and highlights his role as a source of important and influential ideas about the Anglosphere. Churchill's thinking represents an important conduit between Edwardian ideas of empire and citizenship and the years after 1945, when a fixation upon Britain's relative economic decline and doubts about its imperial heritage underpinned the UK's decision to join the EEC. His iconic *History of the English-Speaking Peoples*[1] represented an effort to disseminate visions of British pre-eminence to a broad public. The Anglosphere was now being presented to a mass audience.

While he has become indelibly associated with the lineage of the Anglosphere, Churchill himself did not use this term, preferring to talk of the English-speaking peoples or races. But he is still widely cited as the architect of an Anglosphere tradition that is fundamentally at odds with the idea of UK involvement in an integrated Europe.[2] This appropriation of his mantle remains contentious and can be misleading. Far from being a creator of this lineage, his thinking was a direct descendant of some of the foundational ideas about race, nationhood and citizenship that were assembled in the later years of the nineteenth century.[3] Equally, it was formed out of direct experience of the military and administrative aspects of colonial governance.

Churchill's Empire

Historians continue to debate how important the imperial experience was for Churchill and what exactly were the most important and consistent principles he held on the various issues relating to colonial rule on which he spoke and acted during his career. His political contemporary Leo Amery famously characterised his interest in empire as synthetic and secondary to his much deeper interest in England, a charge repeated by Clement Attlee.[4] In fact, perceptions of Churchill's relationship with empire altered at different stages of his career. It was during the 1920s that he acquired the reputation for being a 'diehard' who was out of step with his colleagues and stuck in a pre-First World War mindset. This view of him returned to the fore as he expressed his opposition to the Attlee government's attempts, after 1945, to make decolonisation an orderly process.[5]

This reputation was confirmed by the support he expressed for the 'forward policy', a position associated with imperial enthusiasts from the nineteenth century. Churchill was known as somebody ready to advocate military action by Britain to defend its imperial interests and willing to break with mainstream orthodoxy in defending such a stance. He urged a firm military response during the 1920s in the face of the growing nationalist movement in India, a position that was seen as defying credibility in official circles. And in 1931 he reacted with fury to the news of negotiations between the viceroy of India and Mahatma Gandhi for a political truce after the latter had launched a campaign of civil disobedience. In an address to the Council of the West Essex Unionist Association, he declared:

> It is alarming and also nauseating to see Mr. Gandhi, an Inner Temple lawyer, now become a seditious fakir of a type well known in the East, striding half-naked up the steps of the Palace, while he is still organizing and conducting a defiant campaign of civil disobedience. ... The truth is that Gandhi-ism and all it stands for will have to be grappled with and finally crushed.[6]

These diehard motifs were important elements in his thinking about India in particular, and the British Empire more generally, but they were not the whole story.[7] Churchill also held with some consistency to several key principles that tended to shape his various judgements about the imperial situations and issues with which he engaged. He undoubtedly retained an intuitive belief in racial hierarchy from the Victorian era and believed resolutely in the cultural superiority of the Anglo-Saxon peoples. But he also held to the broadly liberal conviction that with the blessings of this civilisational inheritance came the duty to behave humanely towards other races. There were also traces in his thinking on empire of the Gladstonian conscience of the previous century and a particularly strong commitment to the importance of Anglo-American civilisation.[8]

The liberal streaks within his outlook help explain Churchill's sharp criticism of overt and counter-productive forms of racial exploitation and violence. Despite some shifts of emphasis and tone and a pragmatic temperament which led him to consider situations on a case-by-case basis, his thinking exhibited considerable continuity in this area. Above all, he was convinced that empire was the necessary condition for British pre-eminence. Even during some of the most pressing moments of the Second World War he was acutely aware of potential threats to colonial interests. In his very first speech to the House of Commons as prime minister, he declared that the British Empire, not Britain alone, would fight to the end against Hitler. And, following the battle of El Alamein, he defiantly declared in the Commons that he had not become the king's first minister to preside over the 'liquidation' of the empire.

His colonial thinking coalesced in the course of several formative, early experiences. The young Churchill became an extremely well-known figure in the English-speaking world, mainly as a result of his work as a military journalist and seeker of adventure. His early posting to India, as a young cavalry officer, afforded his first experience of warfare and led to a deeper, more informed set of reflections about empire on his part. He then travelled as a journalist-cum-soldier to the North West Frontier, where he observed and took part in intensive military action in the mountainous terrain of Afghanistan, and then ventured in the same capacity to Sudan. There, he observed the darker side of British imperialism and came face to face with various acts of violence and brutality. But it was in

South Africa, during the Boer War from 1899 to 1900, that Churchill came to the attention of a much larger audience. Working again as an embedded military reporter, he was captured and made a famous – though not uncontroversial – escape from a prisoner-of-war camp and returned to a hero's welcome in England.[9] The Boers, whose cause was fashionable in the Anglophone world, elicited considerable ambivalence in him. He admired their fortitude and belief in self-government. But, ultimately, he remained steadfast in his commitment to the priority of Britain's imperial interests, an imperative that overrode any call to affinity with another white Christian people 'bringing civilisation' to Africa.

In addition to this early penchant for adventure and self-aggrandisement, Churchill was seen, when he first entered politics, as a figure inclined to favour military modes of thinking. He worked hard to overcome these associations. During his first ministerial position, as undersecretary of state for the colonies from 1905 to 1908, he impressed with his hard work and gift for strategic thinking. Thereafter he was drawn away from colonial issues and deliberately sought to broaden his range of experience and political interests by promoting the cause of domestic social reform on behalf of the working classes. But this cause also had an imperial dimension, as Churchill joined the ranks of those concerned that the unfitness of the working classes represented the gravest threat to Britain's commitment and capacity to retain a great empire.

After leaving the Colonial Office, and following stints as president of the Board of Trade and home secretary, Churchill moved to the position of first lord of the Admiralty in 1911. There he engaged with questions of military strategy and was a keen moderniser of Britain's naval forces in the context of growing competition from Germany. In his eyes the Royal Navy was integral to Britain's supremacy over the world's main sea routes, with the passage to India guarded by its bases at Gibraltar, Malta, Suez and Aden. Conversant with the ideas of Mahan and other naval authorities, Churchill was a keen exponent of the view that sea lanes remained the arterial routes of the world economy, and he argued that, if it was to remain a global power, Britain needed to invest in the requisite hardware to secure pre-eminence in this area.[10]

Churchill returned to the Colonial Office in 1921 and served in Lloyd George's coalition government for another two years. Dogged by criticism that he was heavy-handed in his response to colonial situations, especially in relation to the challenges associated with both Eastern and Southern Africa, he was also an advocate of responsible colonial governance – hence his speech in 1920 on the Armritsar massacre, in which he ably defended the government's censure of General Dyer. In relation to East Africa, he did appear, in this period, to shift towards being more sympathetic to the white settlers seeking to oppose further immigration from Asia. And, even though he was privately critical of this community and their leaders, his stance caused considerable offence in India. But his abiding belief, set out in a keynote address in 1922, was that colonial officials should combine firmness with a sensitivity to local situations and sentiments. He continued to indicate publicly that he did not believe that the goal of introducing democracy was necessarily the right approach to take for many African and Asian peoples, a stance that was to put him on a collision course with American opinion at a later date.

Empire also crossed his path much closer to home. As the Irish question returned once more to the forefront of British politics, following the Easter Rising of 1916 and the war of independence that began in 1919, Churchill acquired a reputation for pragmatism and moderation on this front. He was trenchantly opposed to the Conservative Party's flirtation with Ulster Unionist militarism before 1914 and became an articulate advocate of Home Rule for Ireland in this period. However, as war secretary in 1919, he put his faith in the Royal Irish Constabulary's reserve force – the notorious 'Black and Tans' – which was responsible for a series of atrocities that served to inflame nationalist sentiment in the North. Once a ceasefire was agreed he played a notable role in the negotiations with the Irish leadership and was a strong proponent of the notion of Ireland retaining its dominion status.

Churchill was also required to deal with the unexpected crisis that developed as a result of the defeat of Greek troops by the Turks, which opened up a real threat to the British position at Chanak in 1922. He sided with Lloyd George in calling for a military response to the Turkish threat, a stance that was not supported by other European nations, or by Canada, and was not popular at home. His clumsy handling of this situation confirmed to some – not least his critics in the dominions – that he was an insensitive centraliser when it came to imperial relations. The Chanak incident was an important factor in triggering Arthur Balfour's subsequent definition of Britain and the dominions as 'autonomous Communities within the British Empire'. Rather ironically, Churchill, the great advocate of the shared destiny of the English-speaking peoples, helped propel the politicians of a number of these countries towards support for independence. More generally, the support he expressed privately for the idea of using chemical weapons in warfare, particularly in the context of the Iraqi revolt in the 1920s, reveals much about the depth and character of his commitment to British imperial interests in this period.[11]

After 1945, Churchill remained obdurately reluctant to countenance the winding up of empire and was sharply critical of the Labour government's moves towards decolonisation. His reputation as a diehard on this front now returned, prompted by the repeated accusations of 'scuttling' that he threw at his Labour opponents. He was particularly aggrieved and disappointed by the rapidity with which the prospect of Indian independence became inevitable in the late 1940s, and, with this development, Britain lost what he viewed as its strategic lynchpin and economic jewel. This turn of events created immediate strategic dilemmas for the UK, making it harder to relinquish its position in the Middle East, which now assumed greater importance because India was lost. Nehru's announcement in 1947 that India would become a republic looked like it would jeopardise the prospect of Indian participation in the newly formed Commonwealth. However, this was offset by Labour's swift announcement of dominion status for the country, a decision shaped by the determination to shore up what remained of British influence.

India's independence represented a huge blow to Britain's confidence in its own imperial mission and dented long-established ideas about its global reach and influence. And it opened up an important fault line in political life between those who urged a new statecraft, based upon an acceptance of the need to manage an orderly retreat from empire, and diehards – mostly in the Conservative Party – who preached the case for assertive attempts to maintain Britain's remaining imperial positions; Churchill was in the latter camp. These differing perspectives reflected two increasingly divergent visions within the Tory Party about the nature and future of the British Empire.[12] During the 1930s, figures such as Stanley Baldwin and Neville Chamberlain had come to view it as a growing strain upon British resources and asserted the merits of indirect forms of control, working with local elites to ensure order where possible, and supporting indirect forms of rule. Churchill, on the other hand, was one of a number of voices in the Conservative Party who tended to view with suspicion signs that the British state was softening its commitments to empire.

Yet Churchill's thinking about empire was more fluid than is typically acknowledged. And his linguistic flexibility enabled him to shift between references to empire, Britain's Commonwealth and the Commonwealth of Nations, as the occasion demanded. Over time, and with some reluctance, he gradually came to accept that the British state needed to accommodate the drive to self-government in the colonies in pragmatic ways, and that it needed a statecraft designed to protect its core interests. And one of the main reasons for the pragmatic note that crept into his political thinking on this score was his first-hand experience, during wartime, of the forces eroding Britain's imperial position – its diminished economic strength and growing reliance upon the United States.

Britain Victorious ... but Diminished?

Following the outbreak of the Second World War and Germany's initial military successes in the Low Countries and France, Britain was isolated in Europe, its own national security was at risk, and its colonies were increasingly vulnerable. In this situation, it was imperative that the USA be persuaded once more to join a war in the European theatre, and Churchill, as prime minister, did all he could to ensure that this happened.

Victory for Britain came at a heavy price, as the war took a major toll upon its economy and public finances. And the outlines of a new international order, based upon American pre-eminence, began to emerge in the final years of this conflict. Britain found itself diminished as an international power and heavily dependent upon its American ally, especially in fiscal terms. From 1941 onwards, American offers of financial support to Britain (primarily through the Lend-Lease scheme) were seen as necessary resources to sustain the British war effort but also as sources of leverage as the United States sought to promote its vision of a liberal international order, as well as to ensure that the principle of self-determination, which was set out in the Atlantic Charter of 1941, would be respected by the European imperial powers, especially Britain. As the war progressed, Roosevelt and other American leaders repeatedly raised the prospect of colonies being replaced by new forms of international control and trusteeship.

Churchill came under considerable pressure to renounce the UK's imperial ambitions in exchange for enough money and goods to make it through the war. He managed to avoid making any such commitment, but the UK's growing indebtedness ensured growing dependence on the USA and increased vulnerability to the latter's hostility to the British Empire. As Christopher Hitchens observed, 'almost from the declaration of war against Nazi Germany, Churchill was engaged in a sort of "Second Front," to protect the British Empire, against his putative ally'.[13] At times, disagreements over the hostile stance which Roosevelt and other American politicians adopted towards Britain's imperial interests soured relations between the two leaders. Churchill's repeated rhetorical references to the shared history and future unity of the English-speaking peoples was intended, in part, to elide these differences of outlook and interest.

The Roosevelt administration subscribed to the vision, which had first emerged in the 1930s, of a new economic order which would tear down the tariff barriers and remove the protectionist practices that had inhibited capitalist development in the interwar period. These issues were thrown into relief by the deal struck with the Americans at the Bretton Woods negotiations of 1944, which sought to establish the template for a new economic settlement based upon the convertibility of the dollar and the American ambition to build new global institutions – notably the IMF and the World Bank – under their own tutelage, and indeed on their own soil. The British delegation, led by the celebrity economist John Maynard Keynes, proved unable, in the face of their American counterparts' support for a more extensive liberalisation of the international economy, to make headway with their proposals for an open, world trading system suitably modified to protect Britain's imperial interests: 'At every step to Bretton Woods, the Americans had reminded [the British], in as brutal a manner as necessary, that there was no room in the new order for the remnants of British imperial glory.'[14] The deal agreed at this summit lasted only a short period of time, giving way in 1947 to the Marshall Plan launched by the USA with the goal of reconstructing Western Europe's shattered economies.

The international summits of the final years of the war appeared, symbolically, to place Britain – through the presence of its wartime leader, Churchill – alongside the two other great world powers. But the actual talks, and the deals reached at them, tended in practice to confirm the second-tier status of the UK. The sense that a new balance of power was emerging – in Europe and the wider world – as a result of the pre-eminence and rivalry of these two 'superpowers' was now a defining theme in international relations and was accentuated by the onset of the Cold War.[15] It was increasingly apparent that Britain required American support to maintain some of its key commitments, especially in the Middle East and Asia. But the broader US ambition to peg the economies of the Western world to the dollar, and the attempt to promote an economic order based upon the depth, liquidity and openness of US financial markets, shaped the subsequent era of market-led growth.

This economic vision was closely intertwined with the political imperative from 1943 onwards to contain the Soviet Union and its allies. These goals necessitated American pre-eminence within a newly constructed bloc of Western states, and this required the rapid rehabilitation, after 1945, of West Germany as a key bulwark against Soviet influence. Another by-product of the formation of the 'West' – in direct competition with the USSR-led 'East' – was that Britain now found itself within an international system which significantly restricted its own room for manoeuvre. Any prospect of maintaining a leading role in world affairs was contingent upon establishing a close relationship with the United States. And so the British stood back and watched the baton of world leadership pass to its ally, the culmination of a lengthy process which had first gathered pace during the nineteenth century, and which had at different moments threatened to result in military conflict between these states.

Anglo-America

That it was Churchill who, despite his imperialist proclivi-
ties, effectively presided over the early process of the dissolution of the British Empire is an irony that was not lost
on his political opponents, or on later historians. In his
notable revisionist account, John Charmley suggests that
Churchill's idealistic invocation of Anglo-America shaped
the fateful decision to bind the UK too tightly to American
policies and, as a result, helped accelerate the liquidation
of its own empire.[16] Other historians disagree, stressing the
insuperability of the forces that Churchill was facing and
the overwhelming need to ensure American support; he
was, in the words of one leading historian, 'trapped in
historical processes that they could not control'.[17] A more
pertinent question is whether the grandiloquent presenta-
tion of Anglo-America served to accentuate tensions with
the other English-speaking community that Britain nurtured – the 'white dominion' peoples. Decisions about
military strategy, as well as the negotiation of the post-war
settlement, threw up acute political dilemmas about
whether, and how, these countries should be consulted and
how much autonomy they had in relation to the imperial
metropole. For the most part Churchill sought to achieve
a balance between these attachments, but, in the exigent
circumstances of the war, it was to the American relationship that he turned most assiduously, and anxiously.

Born into a family with roots on both continents,
Churchill championed Anglo-American unity across the
different phases of his career,[18] but it came to acquire much
greater prominence first during the Great War, as he urged
the USA to join with Britain, and then as war loomed
in the 1930s. He framed this deep historical relationship
as the basis for a contemporary partnership that could not
only win the current conflict but also proceed to shape a
new international order within which British imperial
interests would be protected and American ambitions

respected. These two states were now destined to work closely together and serve as guardians of the security and prosperity of the Western world, building a new era of liberal civilisation.

These ideas were given iconic expression in his Harvard graduation speech of September 1943, delivered as the tide of war was beginning to run in the Allies' favour. On this occasion Churchill not only made the case for close strategic cooperation between the two powers but also called for a reimagining of their historic relationship, presenting this as the basis for a more collaborative future. The speech elicited a mixed response in the United States, a reminder that Anglo-America did not have quite the same traction on the other side of the Atlantic. During the course of his visit Churchill floated to sceptical US officials the idea for a scheme to enable a common form of citizenship for residents of the USA and the British Commonwealth countries who might, after a period of residency, come to acquire voting privileges in each other's countries[19] – an idea that has, interestingly, resurfaced in recent Conservative thinking.

The Harvard address forms one part of a pair of notable speeches on Anglo-America. It was followed by his keynote oration at Fulton, Missouri, in 1946. Primarily known for its dramatic depiction of the 'iron curtain' falling across Europe, this also offered an occasion for grand rhetoric about the shared lineage and bright future of the Anglosphere and included the same idealistic call for the reunification of its constituent peoples. They were, Churchill insisted, bound together by a common inheritance – the English tradition of government and the key values of representative government and liberty – which had evolved across several centuries and been transported far and wide by the migration of earlier generations. He now connected this familiar theme with the pressing requirements of the new international situation, presenting the Soviet Union as the paramount threat to democracy and liberty throughout the world. And so he urged the Anglosphere countries, under American leadership, to join the Western alliance. And he employed the phrase that has come to haunt British political thinking ever since as he talked of its 'special relationship' with the United States.

The History of the English-Speaking Peoples

To understand what Churchill meant by this term, and to appreciate why he set so much store upon the prospect of a newly constituted alliance between the USA and Britain after the war, it is necessary to consider carefully how he depicted the English-speaking peoples. This phrase was first aired among a broad community of politicians and thinkers in the USA and Britain who engaged in a broadly liberal debate on the changing role of government in the context of industrialisation during the late nineteenth century.[20] Churchill acquired the habit of depicting this form of imagined community during the 1930s, but he had on various earlier occasions talked up the future unity of the Anglophone races. In 1917, for example, he hailed the decision of the United States to join the Great War as the prelude to the reunification of the Anglo-Saxon world. From an early point in his career it was his habit to invoke the 'English-speaking races', a coinage which reveals the Victorian antecedents of his ideas, and one which was widely employed until the First World War.[21]

It was at this very point that Churchill resumed working on the books which supplied the fullest and most reflective exposition of his thinking on this score – his *History of the English-Speaking Peoples*, published between 1956 and 1958. These volumes represented a concerted attempt to reach a much wider audience on this topic. They were motivated too by his own straightened financial position.[22] The work for them began in 1932 and drew upon the efforts of various historians across these years. Despite the various commitments that distracted Churchill from its completion, and the various hands responsible for the research and drafting it involved, the text bears the clear imprint of his own outlook, historical imagination and prose style.

The volumes provide an accessible and well-paced account of the key episodes and events that form the story of the ineluctable rise of Britain as an exceptional polity and the hub of an expansive, liberal empire. They are replete with dramatic tales of the journeys and achievements of the various settler peoples who carried these political and constitutional ideals across the globe and the countries they formed in England's image. This unusual set of historical volumes, produced under the editorial hand of a living former prime minister, represents the most extensive – and perhaps the most influential – elaboration of the ideals of the Anglosphere produced during the last century. Their impressive sales and the enthusiastic plaudits they elicited testify to their contemporary impact and the celebrity status of their author.

As a contribution to an evolving pattern of Anglospheric discourse, Churchill's contribution was distinguished by his commitment to chart the historical contours of this lineage and his firm belief that the past, properly understood, could undergird a new era of joint Anglo-American hegemony. He stressed both the enduring ties associated with this common inheritance and interconnected history of these peoples and the deep cultural linkages – not least a shared language – which meant that the countries had naturally tended to remain allies and partners. These profound connections occluded the points and periods of disagreement and conflict between them. Despite the war it fought to rid itself of British rule, the USA had forged democratic institutions and a legal system that were broadly congruent with the English lineage, and it had remained faithful to the cultural and political ideals that stemmed from this inheritance. But, Churchill observed, it was now about to take its place in the sun and was the lead partner in the furthering of the civilisational enterprise which the English had begun.

Churchill's volumes were not entirely retrospective in their ambition and were written with one eye on their author's desire to cement the Anglo-American alliance in the post-war period. He implicitly urged the USA not to overlook its deep bonds to its special ally as it sought to establish a new, Western order; and he aimed to remind Britain that its future lay, as in its past, in a close, if informal, relationship with the USA and the 'white dominions'.

The sense of ethnic community evoked in this grand narrative was undoubtedly anchored in the racialised thinking about nations which Churchill had imbibed in his early years. But these works also supplied an updating and reworking of this heritage for the distinct challenges and new sensibilities of the middle years of the century. The replacement of 'races' by 'peoples' is one small, but telling, illustration of Churchill's sensitivity to aspects of the changing cultural environment of mid-century Britain. Yet, in other respects, the books reflected an imperial outlook and geo-political vision which landed in a world that was far more sceptical towards both than it had been when he began working on them. In the mid-1950s, the principle of the equality of races and an abiding scepticism about empire were increasingly prominent themes in official British circles and high politics. And the upbeat, unashamed assertion of Britain's cultural influence in the world, and the celebration of its imperial heritage, tended to strike nostalgic chords that many now disavowed.

European Union

From a contemporary vantage point, Churchill's works are notable in part for what they do not acknowledge – deepening worries about Britain's relative decline. The UK's public policy was still firmly directed to the retention of the protected imperial economic area, which had been a cornerstone of its approach before the war. But a growing chorus of voices from the manufacturing sectors began to

call this stance into question, and the increasing prominence of multinational corporations in the UK economy
increased the weight of argument for free international
trade as opposed to imperial protection. The orthodoxy
that had prevailed up to the late 1940s – that the empire
was the cornerstone of British economic strength – was
now increasingly open to debate. And a growing current
of opinion at elite level began to promote the embryonic
economic union of Western Europe as a plausible alternative option for Britain. Churchill was an important,
though also somewhat ambiguous, contributor to these
early debates.

As the question of the UK's membership of a European
union became a source of major political disagreement
fifty years later, it was to Churchill that leading critics and
proponents of Britain's membership of the EU turned, with
protagonists from both sides claiming him as a posthu-
mous supporter of their cause. This renewal of interest in
his thinking reflects his iconic status among Conservatives
in the years after his death and also says much about the
desire for legitimation on a decision of crucial national
importance. The appearance in mainstream Conservative
circles, from 2010, of a reinvigorated version of the Anglosphere idea was a particular spur to this recent interest.
This dynamic was taken to somewhat absurd lengths by
Boris Johnson MP, whose hagiographic account of
Churchill was widely viewed as an artless attempt to align
himself with the wartime hero's 'brand'.[23]

Whether today's sceptics can credibly claim Churchill as
progenitor and inspiration is the source of much disagreement among contemporary historians. Some of his best-
known pronouncements on this issue were offered in the
unique circumstances of the 1940s, yet references to a
United States of Europe pepper his speeches and writings
from a very early stage in his life and were typically framed
as compatible with some kind of alliance of the English-
speaking peoples. His official biographer notes his reference to this idea in a speech he gave in 1929 in New York

and in an essay he penned in 1930.[24] Yet he was notably ambivalent about this prospect from the outset. In 1932 he urged an American audience that it should 'have no fear of the United States of Europe ... As long as the United States and England grow closer together. Any sinister result could then be properly dealt with.'[25]

According to some historians, far from being the father of Euroscepticism, Churchill is more accurately seen as one of the architects of European Union: 'After the Second World War ... Churchill became the greatest pioneer of the European ideal.'[26] Various pieces of evidence are summoned in support of this judgement. These include his call in Zurich in 1946 for a Franco-German partnership as the first step in building 'a kind of United States of Europe', his founding of the United Europe Movement in 1950, his organisation of the unofficial, but important, Congress of Europe in The Hague, the role he played in lobbying European governments to create the Council of Europe, and his championing of the European Convention on Human Rights in Strasbourg.

Churchill's speech to the Tory Party conference in 1948 also figures prominently in these arguments and is cited by some as a prophetic statement of the importance of the European dimension for the UK.[27] In it he famously identified Britain's unique position as the point where 'three majestic circles' in international relations intersected. He described these in the following terms: 'The first circle for us is naturally the British Commonwealth and Empire, with all that that comprises. Then there is also the English-speaking world in which we, Canada, and the other British Dominions and the United States play so important a part. And finally there is United Europe.'[28]

The terms Churchill selected to characterise these allegiances are telling. For Britain – 'naturally' – empire came first, though he also notably referenced a term of increasingly common usage in the mid-1940s – the 'British Commonwealth' – a tacit recognition that the empire itself might be turning into a rather different entity, with the UK still at its head. Then he referenced the Anglophone world, as a single circle, but with special mention in it of the US relationship. And he finished by asserting the importance of an entity that was not yet in existence – the United States of Europe. The punchline for Churchill was that Britain was the only country that 'has a great part in every one of them' and which is 'the very point of junction'. And, as ever, he rounded off his powerful metaphor with a providentialist assertion of British destiny. If these circles of influence could all be joined together, 'there is no force or combination which could overthrow them or even challenge them.' History provided the basis for Britain's role as a conduit to all of these transnational communities, but so too did geography and the unique way in which empire had allowed the outward-facing and seafaring characteristics of the 'world island' to prosper. It was because Britain was 'at the centre of the seaways and perhaps of the airways' that it had the chance to join these circles.

The vision set out in this speech has shaped the ways in which policy-makers in Britain have thought about its place in the world more than any other delivered since 1945. But its fundamental ambivalence about which of these communities would be most important in the postwar world, and in particular about Europe, are also notable. For critics, Churchill's abiding legacy on this subject was a studied, debilitating ambiguity, which stands in marked contrast to the certitude and consistency of his commitments to the affiliations associated with the Anglosphere.[29] His 1948 speech exudes confidence that Britain could be outside Europe but also deeply engaged with it, and that its tradition of statecraft would ensure that it could manage the tensions bound to arise between these different blocs. In these speeches Churchill presented a vision of European integration which seemed to stretch beyond the economy, encompassing the prospect of military cooperation as well.

But there are good reasons to be wary of the Europhile image of Churchill. There was, as one leading historian has put it, 'a lack of depth in his commitment to European co-operation'.[30] For Churchill, involvement with a prospective European union was secondary to the fundamental focus upon British security and the Anglo-American alliance. And his particular interest in this question in the 1940s most probably reflected his growing concern about whether the USA would remain committed to providing defensive cover to Western Europe in the context of potential Soviet aggression – hence his support for the idea of a common European military capacity. Nothing that Churchill wrote or said in this period committed Britain to substantive economic or military cooperation. Equally, what exactly he meant – in institutional terms – by 'Europe' remained shrouded in ambiguity in these years. Churchill was notably disinclined to offer practical support to the idea of the UK cooperating with the European idea during his final term of office, from 1951 to 1955, when he had several opportunities to do so.[31]

It would appear that the Eurosceptic claim upon Churchill has some foundation. But this too should not be overstated. The kind of stark binary choice between Europe and the Anglosphere, which has become a hallmark of latter-day Euroscepticism, was entirely alien to the Churchillian mindset. For good or ill, he believed that the strategic priorities of the special relationship with the United States and the retention of imperial influence could – indeed, should – be seen as congruent with a friendly disposition towards, and possible cooperation with, an emerging European bloc. The largely hypothetical conjectures of these years soon gave way in British politics to a much more concrete discussion of the pros and cons of the UK's membership of the EEC. During the 1960s a good deal of this debate focused upon the economic worth of the UK's reliance upon Commonwealth markets, which were no longer as profitable as they had previously been. And, increasingly, the European choice emerged as a more sharply defined option in the context of a developing concern about the relative under-performance of the UK economy in comparison with its West European counterparts. Increasingly, the imperial lineage which Churchill had so powerfully championed came to be seen as outmoded and as one source of the kind of golden ageism which was increasingly blamed for holding Britain back. As modernisation – of both economy and society – became the watchword in British politics, the European option found a growing number of supporters, especially in Churchill's own party, as the route to greater economic opportunity and geo-political clout for the UK after empire.

Loyalty to the Commonwealth idea was still a key point of reference and a meaningful attachment for many and was widely referenced in the campaign against the UK's membership of the EEC in 1975. But it was a diminishing force as a carrier of the ethos of the Anglosphere. Over time, as the various ties with former colonies began to weaken, the case made by those arguing for Britain to reinvent and modernise as a European power grew stronger, even though the Commonwealth and the English-speaking peoples remained an important residual source of imagined community for many Britons.

But from the late 1940s, as growing numbers of people from Britain's former's colonies began to make their way to Britain, invoking the reciprocal implications of imperial citizenship, the empire moved back home. Successive waves of immigrants from Africa, Asia and the Caribbean arrived, and this gradually engendered profound concerns in the host population about whether Britain needed to detach from the Commonwealth in order to preserve its English heritage and identity. Increasingly, it came to be seen as a portal through which various alien peoples could enter the country, and a reactive current of sentiment began to gather around a more tightly drawn, insular sense of the nation. Towards the end of his own career, Churchill was troubled by the emergence of immigration as a popular concern in Britain and expressed considerable scepticism about whether the indigenous population would tolerate mass immigration from the non-white peoples of the

Commonwealth. In conversation in 1954 he remarked about the problems that 'will arise if many coloured people settle here. Are we to saddle ourselves with colour problems in the UK?'[32]

Conclusions

During the middle decades of the last century, the decline of the British Empire was widely viewed as irreversible, although politicians and political parties continued to argue, often sharply, over how quickly decolonisation should happen, how the British state should manage this process, and how its relationships with its former colonies should be arranged. But this gathering realisation injected two broad questions into high politics. What was the scope and basis for British power in the world if empire was gone? And what role should Britain play in the new world order that was emerging out of the ashes of the Second World War? Churchill played an immensely influential role by providing influential answers to these questions and by informing the strategic thinking and geo-political assumptions of subsequent generations of politicians. The vision he set out in 1948 of the concentric circles which Britain alone could join together proved beguiling and elusive for a political establishment both dealing with the ongoing fallout from the gradual end of empire and preoccupied by the prospect of relative economic decline. His conviction that the UK could gain leverage and influence as the bridge between the USA and Europe while also nurturing its Commonwealth ties became the unspoken, governing framework shaping the foreign policy outlook of most of the party leaders and prime ministers who came after him.

But Churchill's legacy has been paradoxical in two particular respects. First, he oversaw Britain's contribution to victory in a punishing world conflict. Being on the winning side served to obscure the underlying truth that the expansion of England was now in reverse, a process that had been in motion for many years, starting with the partition of Ireland in 1921. Churchill's capacity to weave inspiring visions of English-speaking union and Anglo-American hegemony enabled some in the British political establishment to avoid thinking too hard about the radically altered circumstances now facing the UK.

Equally, his thinking on some key issues was notably ambivalent – on European union above all. Making reference to a prospective United States of Europe was as much a rhetorical flourish as it was a grand design on his part – at least until the late 1940s. And, even then, Churchill showed little inclination to involve Britain deeply in this process. Over subsequent decades many in his own party came to believe that the European and Anglophone destinies represented divergent, antithetical paths and that Britain had to choose between them in order to prosper. What to his mind were pillars upon which great power status depended came to look like two alternative lifeboats for a country that was starting to slip down the league table of leading Western states. Staving off decline, rather than asserting the country's standing in the world, was increasingly the preoccupation of Britain's ruling elite.

Out of power after 1945, Churchill attempted to provide a wide-ranging, popular understanding of Britain's place in the world by recycling the ideals and story-lines of Anglo-America and the 'kith and kin' relationship with the white peoples of empire. But, even as his idealised portrait of these affiliations hit the bookshops of Britain, the sense of continuity with the pre-war world which he so keenly evoked was starting to fade.

3

A Parting of the Ways: Britain and the Commonwealth in the Post-War World

In a memorandum to his cabinet colleagues in October 1949, the foreign secretary, Ernest Bevin, laid out how the geo-political landscape had shifted in the immediate post-war period and what this meant for the UK. The alliance of Great Britain, the USA and the Soviet Union that won the war had not survived long. The division of Europe and of Germany into East and West, the Berlin Blockade and the formation of NATO had inaugurated an era of super-power rivalry, not cooperation in the pursuit of peace. This, Bevin argued, had left some searching for a 'Third Power' in Europe to stand independently in world affairs alongside Washington and Moscow. But this was a false prospectus, he argued. Western Europe was not strong enough, economically or militarily, to stand up to the Soviet Union alone, as the Berlin crisis had proved. Nor could Britain and her Commonwealth supply the necessary strength. Political divisions, both within the Commonwealth and with Europe, would prevent their consolidation into a coherent third force in world politics. The only option worth pursuing, in the interests of European unity and Commonwealth solidarity, Bevin concluded, was 'the closest association with the United States' and a 'consolidated West'.[1]

The emergence of the 'West' as an ideological and geo-political construct in the years after the Second World War reflected the overwhelming economic and military superiority achieved by the USA and the development of a new Cold War strategy to cement it. Between 1939 and 1945, the US economy roughly doubled in size and surged ahead, while its industrial rivals were left exhausted or defeated. Lend-Lease loans to keep the British economy afloat during the war had been made on terms that left no doubt that the United States would redraw the global economic order once the fighting came to an end, calling time on the sterling area and the British Empire's protected markets. These were to be opened up to US capital in a liberalised regime firmly under American leadership. There was to be one world capitalist system, not a series of competing blocs.

Having paid a huge price for its victory, Great Britain was in no position to dictate terms to the USA. It was massively indebted and had run down its assets. When President Truman abruptly announced the end of Lend-Lease in 1945, Keynes described Britain as facing 'financial Dunkirk'. He was dispatched to Washington to seek US financial assistance and returned with a dollar loan that came with the sterling area's death certificate attached to it. Sterling was to become freely convertible in 1947 and import controls were to be scrapped, moves which finally opened up the British Empire to American exports.

As it turned out, the British economy could not withstand convertibility when it duly arrived in the summer of 1947. A full-blown sterling crisis ensued and dollar convertibility had to be suspended within weeks, followed by further rationing of food and petrol. The alternative option – of severe deflation to restore Britain's balance of payments – could not be countenanced, since it would mean sacrificing full employment and the building of the New Jerusalem on which the Attlee government was embarked. But the suspension of convertibility had to be acceptable to the USA, since it was being asked to continue to allow the sterling area to remain protected, with imperial tariff preferences, import controls on dollar goods, and a currency that could not be freely exchanged – 'precisely those things that American leaders had been so determined to crush eighteen months earlier.'[2]

American forbearance when Britain defaulted on its loan terms was based on a new strategic assessment of the USA's economic and military interests. Without strong economic growth, Britain, the Commonwealth and Western Europe could not trade with America. The 'dollar gap' between the currency needed to import vital US goods and that which they could earn through exports was too wide. Marshall Aid, which channelled billions of dollars to Western Europe to secure its economic recovery, plugged this gap and linked aid receipt to the purchase of US goods. It bought security too. Economic development in Western Europe would underpin the containment of communism to the east, just as Japanese recovery would help secure the Pacific. By giving latitude and aid to its Cold War partners, the USA undergirded the resilience of the postwar economic order it had created.

The idea of a 'West' or 'free world' ranged against the Soviet Union and its satellite states led the United States to dispense with the residues of Anglo-Saxonism, even while Britain remained its most important military partner. Henceforth, the Anglosphere would need to be subsumed within a global set of military and economic alliances, across Europe, Latin America, Africa, the Middle East and Asia – strategic zones through which the fault lines of the Cold War would run. These alliances could not be ideologically founded on a shared Anglo-Saxon history of institutions or language, let alone race. Instead, enunciating a doctrine with which he would become synonymous, Truman spoke in 1947 of 'free peoples' or 'freedom-loving peoples' resisting 'totalitarian regimes'.

Critically for the UK, this reorientation marked the beginning of a longer term conversion on the part of the United States to support for the unification of Europe as a bulwark, first against the Soviet Union and then, later, against post-communist Russia. The USA had three specific reasons for supporting Western European integration, a key objective behind which it threw considerable diplomatic weight.[3] First, integration would permit a reconciliation of France's security needs with West Germany's economic recovery, an ambition that would bear direct fruit in the Schuman plan for a European Coal and Steel Community. Second, the integration of the economies of Western Europe, particularly through a Customs Union, would generate higher levels of trade, investment and productivity growth. In turn, economic prosperity would deliver the resources needed to bind Europe's working classes into Western welfare capitalism and secure its external defence against the Soviet Union. Third, US aid to Western Europe would ultimately pay for itself: Europe's paymasters in Congress would eventually see the returns, not just in the closing of the dollar gap but in the creation of a zone of economic growth stripped of nationalist protectionism and open to US trade and investment.

These basic moorings of US policy would remain remarkably consistent throughout the 1950s as the new institutions of the emerging European Communities took shape. Pragmatism would dictate compromise along the way, and the grandeur of the vision of a United States of Europe that some US policy-makers saw reflected back to them across the Atlantic – and which Churchill stoked in his set-piece European speeches of the late 1940s – would dim with time. Yet compromises over trade, tariffs and currency convertibility were only short-term sacrifices – ones the USA was prepared to make in order to secure the creation of an economic and political order that guaranteed the maintenance of Western capitalist democracy.

The State Department rapidly realised that Great Britain would not lead the process of European integration, however. Although Churchill's enormous prestige, rhetorical brilliance and diplomatic guile succeeded in laying the foundations for a political movement towards pan-Western European unity, the Attlee government saw no reason to choose between Britain's imperial possessions, greater European engagement and its relationship with the USA. Like other governments of the post-war era, it had two overriding objectives: military security and sustained economic growth to pay for the creation of the welfare state. It embraced decolonisation where it had to – most importantly in India – but elsewhere it sought to defend Britain's imperial role and the assets underpinning it. This was an exhausting enterprise which reflected an under-estimation of the economic burdens of maintaining a global imperial position, as well as the long-term consequences of standing aside from the developing process of European integration. But insofar as it constituted a 'worldwide' national strategy, it was, as the economic historian Alan Milward argued, rooted in a reasonable assessment of the costs and benefits of the UK's global position. This strategy helped secure extensive protected markets and a sterling area that was financially integrated into the City of London, political influence in Africa and Asia, albeit on diminished terms, and close relations with the USA. In Milward's words, these were 'the bargaining counters which the United Kingdom had to hand to attain its post-war objectives' and to 'give them away for nothing would have been a foolish and expensive indulgence.'[4]

Keeping Afloat: the UK and the Commonwealth after the Second World War

Britain's post-war recovery depended critically on the Commonwealth and the colonies. The creation of the sterling area and a system of imperial tariffs in the 1930s, coupled with the turn towards protectionism in the USA and Europe, followed by the exigencies of the war economy had produced a dramatically different pattern of international economic activity to that which had characterised the British Empire in the Edwardian era. In the late 1940s over 50 per cent of British exports went to the Commonwealth and colonies, compared with only 10 per cent each for Western Europe and the USA and Canada (which had its own dollar currency) combined. Commonwealth imports to the UK were largely duty free, ensuring that British food supplies could be cheaply bought without using dollars. Britain took nearly three-quarters of New Zealand's exports, two-thirds of West Africa's and nearly 40 per cent of Australia's. Oil supplies from British-owned Middle Eastern concessions were also critical, since they reduced dependence on American imports and gained dollar revenue. Colonies were directly exploited: their commodities could be bought and exported outside the sterling area, building up Britain's dollar reserves, while their manufacturing imports could be constrained. And although the City of London had lost the pivotal global role it had played in the heyday of British imperialism, one-third of all world trade was still invoiced in sterling. The City's capital markets were an indispensable source of capital for the Commonwealth, while a protected sterling area enabled an expansionist, cheap money economic policy to be followed at home.

The centrality of the Commonwealth and colonies to Britain's post-war economic survival ensured that they retained deep cross-party support. Proponents of European integration did not ask the British political elite to choose between imperial loyalties and engagement in Europe. 'Great Britain has an important role to play as a member of the European Union; she has another role as a member of the British Commonwealth. There is nothing inconsistent or incongruous in this', the United Europe Movement argued.[5] For imperialists such as Leo Amery, who had dedicated a lifetime to the cause of imperial unity, Britain was both a world island at the heart of an empire and 'a nation of the European family intimately linked with Europe throughout our whole history'.[6] He swung wholeheartedly behind Churchill's European cause, exploiting the studied ambiguities in his friend's grand vision to endorse a leadership role for Britain and the Commonwealth in the construction of a united Europe. 'We owe it to ourselves as well as to Europe to give a lead on this issue', he argued.[7]

Amery's position was tinged with a declining empire's jealousy of its rising rival. Britain could not 'sacrifice our own trade and employment at home or the strength and unity of the Empire in order to promote American economic imperialism', he wrote. It could not subscribe to 'a doctrine of an uncontrolled world economy'.[8] Amery still conceived of the Commonwealth as an integrated economic bloc, not a string of nations opening up to American trade. Yet, when push came to shove, neither would Amery endorse British integration into a federal Europe. His hierarchy was clear: empire first, then Europe. Voluntary association on the British model, not federalism, should define European unity.

The Conservative high command, which tracked their leader's manoeuvres in Europe warily, was similarly conflicted. Harold Macmillan and Anthony Eden had nodded towards European federation during the war years and shared Churchill's belief that Britain's destiny lay in leading in both Europe and the empire. But these commitments did not translate into an endorsement of European federalism; while deploring the Labour government's rejection of the Schuman Plan, the Conservative leadership did not accept the pooling of sovereignty in a supranational authority which it implied. It put forward alternative proposals for intergovernmental coordination of coal and steel in Europe, but these were rebuffed by Schuman, forcing Churchill to promote plans for a European army instead. Although Churchill gained support for his proposals on the continent, the British government rejected these, arguing that European participation in NATO rendered a European army redundant. When it came to drafting the Conservative manifesto for the 1951 election, Churchill placed working towards a 'United Europe' below the

higher priorities of ensuring the 'safety, progress and cohesion of the British Empire and Commonwealth of Nations'
and 'the unity of the English-speaking peoples, who
together number hundreds of millions.'[9]

Labour was little different. Occasional statements aside,
its post-war leaders were largely hostile to the idea of
European integration. The party's federalists were thin
on the ground, and, when Labour MPs expressed pro-
European positions, these were often motivated by anti-
American sentiments.[10] Bevin worked hard to construct a
new Western European order after the war, but he sought
its unity on Britain's terms and, when he could not secure
these, frustrated the efforts of Churchill's United Europe
activists and their continental counterparts. He rejected
federation and the idea of a written European constitution, which he considered inimical to British traditions
of parliamentary sovereignty and voluntary association
with the dominions. The codified constitutional checks
and balances of post-war European democracies, framed
to inhibit any backsliding to fascism, were not needed
in Britain. His views coincided with those of the bulk of
his party. Herbert Morrison, standing in for Bevin as the
foreign secretary neared his death, famously declared that
the Durham miners 'wouldn't wear' the Schuman coal
and steel plan, and, in a foretaste of the Euroscepticism
that was to become dominant in the Labour Party until
the mid-1960s, the party's National Executive Committee
(NEC) declared its opposition to a federal European state.
An NEC policy statement in 1950 argued that complete
political union would mean a permanent 'anti-Socialist
majority' and an unacceptable degree of uniformity in
national policies. Nor was it simply socialist ambitions
that stood in the way of deeper European integration.
Ties of 'kith and kin' also did. 'In every respect', the NEC
declared, 'we in Britain are closer to our kinsmen in Australia and New Zealand on the far side of the world than
we are to Europe. We are closer in language and origins,
in social habits and institutions, in political outlook and

in economic interest.'[11] Joseph Chamberlain himself could have penned these words.

British policy-makers in the 1950s rejected attempts to reconfigure the Commonwealth into two tiers, comprising an inner 'white club' and an outer circle of 'black' states. The risk that newly independent states would secede if offered second-class status in the Commonwealth was too great.[12] But, in practice, a distinction was drawn on defence and intelligence issues, on which the inner club of old Anglosphere friends worked together, and in foreign policy, where the interests of new and old Commonwealth members diverged sharply.[13] Britannic national loyalties in the white settler Commonwealth also remained strong, nurtured by sustained migration flows between Great Britain and the dominions. Ties of sentiment, often bolstered by overt racism, were particularly potent in Australia and New Zealand. Australia's long-serving post-war prime minister, Robert Menzies, was a romantic monarchist who declared himself 'British to his boot straps'. Support for the British Empire was the lodestar of his foreign policy, and he staunchly maintained it, even as he negotiated Australia's place within the USA's Pacific security umbrella (in 1951, to the UK's intense irritation, Australia and New Zealand took their place in the US constellation of Cold War alliances by signing the ANZUS Pact). Although, in the post-war era of full employment, Australia's labour supply needs could no longer be met by British migrants, it nonetheless maintained a 'white' immigration policy that lasted into the 1970s (the post-war Labour immigration minister, Arthur Calwell, notoriously declared when he deported Chinese refugees in 1947 that 'Two Wongs don't make a White').

New Zealand's British identity was perhaps even stronger, underpinned by a consistent flow of expats – known, as in Australia, as Ten Pound Poms – from the mother country. Nearly 200,000 Britons migrated to New Zealand in the 1950s, most of them English and Scottish by birth. 'Right up to the 1960s', writes Belich, 'Britain was still the major source of imports, export receipts, investment, technology, culture and immigrants. The cars in the street were British, as were the postage stamps and the governor-general.'[14] Defence of the Suez imperial trade route was critical for New Zealand, and, when it came to the cease-fire resolution on the crisis at the United Nations General Assembly in 1956, Australia and New Zealand alone voted with Britain, France and Israel.

The position was different in Canada. Its economic and geo-political coordinates had shifted during the war as a result of its dependency on the USA for bilateral aid. It continued to draw migrants from the UK and to benefit from imperial trade preferences, but its southern neighbour was now a magnetic economic force, and trade flows between Canada and the USA were buttressed by enormous US investment in the development of Canada's infrastructure, natural resources and industrial capacity. By 1955, the US share of foreign capital invested in Canada was 77 per cent, compared with 17 per cent for Britain, reversing the ratios that had existed at the beginning of the century. Canada was a staunch supporter of NATO and the Western alliance, but it was sympathetic to anti-imperialist sentiment in Asia and Africa and keen to nurture political links with the emerging non-aligned movement. It would not follow the mother country wherever it led, and, after Eisenhower had brought Britain to heel over Suez, Lester Pearson, Canada's foreign secretary in the 1950s and a future prime minister, broke imperial ranks, stitching together a coalition at the United Nations that included India and the USA to achieve a diplomatic end to the stand-off. The crisis, Pearson said, had 'brought the Commonwealth to the verge of dissolution'.[15]

It was South Africa, the nursery of the Round Table movement, which would make the first complete break with the Anglosphere. In 1948 it elected an Afrikaner nationalist government that set about building the apartheid regime. Trade ties – including controversial arms sales from the UK – remained strong, and investment from

Britain flowed into Southern African mining and industrial interests. But the consolidation of apartheid and Afrikaner republicanism brought a waning of Britannic sentiment in South Africa on the one hand (although British allegiances remained important in the former imperial colonies, particularly in Natal province)[16] and a wave of repulsion in the rest of the Commonwealth on the other. Irredentist British Conservatives continued to support white supremacism in Southern Africa, but relations between the two countries became increasingly strained. In 1957, South Africa abolished the Union Jack and *God Save the Queen*, and in 1960 it voted to become a republic. That same year, with the support of Great Britain, the Sharpeville massacre elicited condemnation of the apartheid regime from the UN. South Africa was promptly forced out of the Commonwealth by a coalition of African states, India and Canada. By the time it was readmitted in 1994, the Commonwealth had long ceased to exist as a meaningful political and economic entity.

These developments ensured that, over the course of the 1950s, Britain's relationship with the Commonwealth and its remaining colonies, and also with the USA, were transformed. The 'winds of change' that Harold Macmillan had caught blowing through Africa would herald the final days of empire. The Suez crisis, and the brutal demonstration of Britain's financial and military subservience to the USA which it supplied, began to bring home to Britain's political elite the economic and political costs of imperial overstretch. And the unfolding economic miracle of Les Trente Glorieuses in Western Europe, which had gathered pace in the 1950s, exposed the relative decline of the British economy and the penalties – in manufacturing competitiveness, export market access and political influence – of staying outside the EEC after the Treaty of Rome was signed in 1957. Between 1950 and 1960, GDP grew at an annual average of 2.7 per cent in the UK, compared with 7.75 per cent in West Germany, 5.85 per cent in Italy and 4.6 per cent in France. By the early

1960s, productivity levels in West Germany and France had overhauled those in the UK, and they have remained higher ever since. It was this relative economic decline that would finally prompt Britain to turn decisively towards Europe.[17]

The Halting Turn to Europe

Nonetheless, the Commonwealth continued to dominate British thinking about how to engage with the processes of economic integration that were taking place in Western Europe. After a halting start, events moved swiftly in this arena, including the decision at the Messina conference of foreign ministers of the 'Six' in 1955 to examine proposals for a common market, the resolution of differences between France and Germany in 1956 on how the market would work, and the signing of the Treaty of Rome in 1957 establishing the EEC. Standing aside from these developments put Britain at some disadvantage. It faced tariff penalties accessing a large and rapidly growing market, its competitors were likely to benefit from trade liberalisation and economies of scale within the new market, and the Six were soon to become a powerful force in world trade negotiations. Yet the overwhelming view among Britain's ministers and mandarins remained in favour of keeping the UK out. The primary reason for this was the worry that joining would weaken the deep relationship Britain had with the Commonwealth and the former colonies. If Britain joined, these countries might well find themselves subject to tariffs on their exports to the UK, which would not apply to goods from the Six. Reciprocal preferences for British manufactured goods would then be lost.

In place of the EEC, Britain put forward a plan – Plan G – for a European Free Trade Area, excluding agriculture. This was, initially, fiercely contested within the cabinet, but after the debacle of Suez, when ministers needed to find new grounds for national and political unity, the government rallied around it. It was consistent with the UK's orientation towards worldwide trade liberalisation, broadly acceptable to the Commonwealth, and had some support on the continent. But it went nowhere. France blocked it, both for domestic economic reasons and for fear of the UK using the free trade proposal to secure political leadership of Europe and, with it, US dominance over Europe. The UK was left to form a free trade association (EFTA) among those Western European countries that were still outside the EEC. This development, however, had little impact on the Six.

In Milward's analysis of the cabinet papers of this period, the word 'Commonwealth' evokes 'so rich a tapestry of loyalty and cultural similarity, spread so enduringly around the globe, that the quietly prosperous balance of domestic politics need never be troubled if relations with the Commonwealth were left undisturbed.' This was an increasingly unreal worldview, inherited from the pre-war Chamberlainites, kept alive not just by the Empire Loyalists in the Conservative Party, but also by One Nation social reformers like RAB Butler, who 'supported a mixture of domestic and imperial policies which they believed made any compromise with a European common market either irrelevant, or a disastrously false step.'[18]

By the early 1960s, such views had lost ground. The EEC had been successfully established, and it had considerable US support. President Kennedy wanted the UK to join so as to provide a counterweight to France. Continued influence on US strategic policy therefore demanded re-engagement with Europe. There had been a shift in the balance of economic considerations as well: not only had the EEC economies outperformed the UK, but the share of Britain's exports going to the Commonwealth and colonies had declined substantially after 1958, when sterling finally became convertible with the dollar and other currencies. This had driven up demand for British exports in North America and, more sharply, in the newly formed

EEC. West Germany was now the UK's fourth biggest export market, and the share of British exports taken by the EEC was now approaching 20 per cent.

The British government thus took the decision to open negotiations to secure entry to the EEC. Announcing the government's position to the House of Commons, the prime minister, Harold Macmillan, posed this question:

> ... how can we best serve the Commonwealth? By standing aside from the movement for European unity, or by playing our full part in its development? By retaining our influence in the New World, or by allowing it to decline by the relative shrinking of our own political and economic power compared with the massive grouping of the modern world? Britain in isolation would be of little value to our Commonwealth partners, and I think that the Commonwealth understands it. It would, therefore, be wrong in my view to regard our Commonwealth and our European interests as conflicting. Basically, they must be complementary.[19]

Macmillan had pivoted to the view that continued relative economic decline would imperil Britain's political leadership of the Commonwealth and its status as a global power. Without a stronger, more dynamic economy and a position of political influence inside the EEC, Britain's international position was at risk. The Commonwealth and remaining colonies could no longer supply the economic muscle to undergird British power; nor could her influence on the USA be guaranteed while she stood outside the decision-making structures emerging in Western Europe. Churchill's circles could not be squared unless Britain joined in the great project of European economic integration.

Yet, in practical terms Macmillan had not accepted that Britain should seek membership on terms that would mean abandoning Commonwealth tariff preferences. That choice was faced a year later after lengthy negotiations, during which the Six, particularly France, proved unwilling to admit Britain with 'comparable outlets' for Commonwealth exports. When it first sought entry to the EEC, the UK did so with all of its Commonwealth baggage attached, and this was still quite considerable. The 'Old Commonwealth' still depended heavily on British markets. In 1960, nearly 24 per cent of Australia's exports went to the UK, as did over half of New Zealand's and 15.8 per cent of Canada's. Much of this was agricultural produce that sustained politically powerful farming lobbies and rural interests. Commonwealth governments fought hard to protect these interests, supported by vociferous elements within the British press.

India and the 'New Commonwealth' countries posed different challenges. India, Ceylon and Pakistan warned of serious risks to their exports and of the moral obligations of the UK and the Six to help them develop. But, like the newly independent states of Africa, they were resistant to anything, particularly Associated Overseas Territory status in relation to the EEC, which smacked of colonialism. In the end, British negotiators failed both Old and New Commonwealth alike. Edward Heath, leading the negotiations with the Six for Britain, was forced to concede that there would be neither general agreement to secure 'comparable outlets' for Old Commonwealth exports nor principled, rather than specific, terms for the rest of Britain's colonies and New Commonwealth partners.

Reflecting the needs of Antipodean agricultural exporters, North American manufacturers, the commercial interests of Asian city-states such as Singapore and Hong Kong, West Indian and African commodity producers, and the needs of populous but poor countries such as India and Pakistan was a gargantuan task for Britain's negotiators. And Britain's attempt to incorporate these relationships in its bargaining position ultimately failed, as De Gaulle vetoed Britain's application. The 'great escort' of Commonwealth countries it brought with it were an important factor in this decision. In De Gaulle's view, the Commonwealth and colonies weighed heavily on Britain's allegiances, and their widely divergent economic interests could not be aligned with those of the EEC.

On the Conservative backbenches, Commonwealth sympathies, rather than objections to the loss of parliamentary sovereignty, formed the wellspring of Eurosceptic opposition to Macmillan's policy. Sovereignty barely featured as an issue, either in the official mind or in the wider political debate. In part, this was because ministers deliberately chose to downplay it; Edward Heath, in particular, preferred to let 'the sleeping dog' of sovereignty lie.[20] De Gaulle's open hostility to European federalism also contrived to reduce its prominence as a concern. Only Lord Kilmuir, the lord chancellor, pointed unequivocally to the transfer of sovereignty implied by signing the Treaty of Rome: parliament and the British courts would inevitably surrender certain powers over economic affairs to the EEC. He wanted the fullest public awareness of the constitutional consequences of joining the EEC, so that those opposed to entry would not seize on them with more damaging effect later on. This was a 'prophetic warning, as to which, after many years of relatively acquiescent silence, there grew up some of the most bitter arguments.'[21] When Britain sought entry for a third time in the early 1970s, the issue of sovereignty – and the related question of securing a popular mandate for entering Europe – could no longer be put aside.

For its part, the Labour Party remained largely Eurosceptic. It now included a growing band of pro-Europeans, led by Roy Jenkins, but they would become politically decisive only in the early 1970s, when Edward Heath relied on their support to take the UK into the EEC. In the early 1960s, the weight of opinion in the Labour Party was still opposed to Common Market membership and supportive, for both sentimental and principled reasons, of the Commonwealth. Hugh Gaitskell, the Labour leader, was, in turns, indifferent and irritated by the European question. He was fighting internal battles on the terrain of nuclear disarmament and public ownership, and Europe was an unwelcome complication.[22]

Lecturing at Harvard in the late 1950s, Gaitskell argued that there 'were deep and profound reasons' why the UK would not join a political federation in Europe. First and foremost was the fact that Great Britain was at the centre of the Commonwealth, a relationship which he depicted not as imperialistic, but as the exact opposite: 'We are proud that out of a colonial Empire there has been and is being developed an association of free, independent, self-governing states, containing many different races, colours, and religions.'[23] At its best, this was an expression of a moral commitment to decolonisation, racial equality and global poverty reduction that was deeply felt in parts of the Labour movement. But its limits were apparent. Gaitskell still thought of Great Britain as the 'mother country' of the Commonwealth, shorn of which it would be reduced to a 'Little England' that would cease to have a 'special relationship' with the United States. He would harden this line until it formed the emotional core of his speech to the 1962 Labour Party conference, when he argued that entry to a European federation 'means the end of a thousand years of history ... [and] the end of the Commonwealth'. 'How can one really suppose', he said, that, 'if the mother country, the centre of the Commonwealth, is a province of Europe (which is what federation means) it could continue to exist as the mother country of a series of independent nations. It is sheer nonsense.'[24]

The sharpest riposte to Gaitskell's worldview, and that of his peers, would come from Dean Acheson, the former US secretary of state, who famously remarked at West Point in December 1962 that 'Great Britain has lost an Empire and not yet found a role.' It is worth considering the rest of the paragraph in which this iconic quotation sits, in which Acheson proceeded to diagnose Britain's post-imperial malaise and to demolish the delusion that the Commonwealth equipped it with a powerful geo-political place in the world:

The attempt to play a separate power role – that is, a role apart from Europe, a role based on a 'special relationship' with the United States, a role based on being the head of a 'Commonwealth' which has no political structure, or unity, or strength, and enjoys a fragile and precarious economic relationship by means of the sterling area and preferences in the British market – this role is about played out.[25]

The End of the Anglo-World

In the course of the 1960s this blunt assessment was borne out. Trade between Great Britain and the Commonwealth continued the pattern of relative decline set by currency convertibility in the late 1950s. In 1962, the Commonwealth took nearly 30 per cent of the UK's exported goods and provided a similar proportion of her imports. A decade later, each was a little over a fifth, proportions that would fall further in the 1970s. Australia and New Zealand, in particular, took the cue from Great Britain's efforts to negotiate entry to the EEC and diversified their exports. In contrast, Western European markets grew in importance for Great Britain: Germany, France, the Netherlands and Ireland steadily overtook the Britannic Anglosphere in trade ties. By 1980, Canada, Australia and New Zealand had all dropped out of the UK's top ten countries for the import and export of goods.

The turbulent economic environment of the mid-1960s also brought pressure to bear on Commonwealth investment and Britain's global ambitions. Buffeted by a succession of balance of payments and sterling crises, Harold Wilson's Labour government sought to direct savings into domestic industrial growth and to constrain overseas capital investment into the main sterling area economies. Simultaneously, public spending on the welfare state increased substantially, as Labour delivered on its plans for expanding education and social security. Yet, upholding the value of sterling and reassuring creditors while maintaining full employment and expanding the welfare state served only to expose the cost of maintaining Britain's global defence commitments, which in 1965 still stood at 7 per cent of GDP. In steps and stages, under pressure from sterling crises in particular, the government agreed to reduce defence spending east of Suez, bringing an end to the British military presence in Malaysia and Singapore on a phased timetable. However, even then the economic policy of maintaining sterling could not hold: the pound was devalued in 1967, and the new chancellor, Roy Jenkins, used the aftershocks that resulted as a mechanism to enforce a reduction of military commitments in Asia and the Gulf. Britain's military reach to the last remnants of Asian empire and Antipodean Anglosphere was brought to an end. Henceforth, there would be no British bases outside Europe and the Mediterranean. Announcing the policy to the House of Commons at the beginning of 1968, Wilson remarked on Kipling's *Recessional Hymn*: 'Far-called, our navies melt away; / On dune and headland sinks the fire: / Lo, all of our pomp of yesterday / Are one with Nineveh and Tyre!'[26]

Wilson entered Downing Street in 1964 with the warm wishes of the Commonwealth ringing in his ears. But the long-drawn-out crisis in Rhodesia that quickly ensued, and the bitter rows it provoked, whittled away at this store of goodwill. Brute economics administered a healthy dose of realism. Having inherited Gaitskell's instinctive scepticism towards Europe, Wilson gradually turned towards the EEC, just as his predecessors had done. He found the path blocked by De Gaulle again. But, by the late 1960s, industrial strife, the strains in the post-war economic settlement, and the final curtain for empire convinced much of the British establishment of the attractions of joining the European market. The election of a committed pro-European Conservative prime minister and the death of De Gaulle in 1970 would pave the way for Britain finally to enter the EEC.

The third round of negotiations for entry would hinge on the position of the new French president, Georges

Pompidou. The Commonwealth remained a sticking point. The French were concerned that sterling balances held in London and sterling's reserve currency status were a risk to the EEC, since they exposed the UK to global obligations and to balance of payments and exchange rate crises that might drag in the Six if the UK joined the Common Market (under the terms of the Treaty of Rome, exchange rates were a matter of common concern). The global status of the dollar and sterling, and the associated problems of balance of payments between the USA and the UK as deficit countries, on the one hand, and the Six as surplus countries, on the other, had been a longstanding source of friction in the 1960s, and the sterling issue had proved a headache in each of the previous British applications to join the EEC. Moreover, repeated sterling crises appeared to reveal weaknesses in the British economy that the stiff winds of Common Market competition would only exacerbate, at least in the short term.

This time, however, the issue did not prove intractable. The sterling area had been progressively diminished during the 1960s by the unilateral withdrawal of a number of African countries and diversification from sterling of the foreign reserves of countries such as Australia. Moreover, after the 1967 devaluation, Britain had struck an agreement with the USA to offer guarantees against 90 per cent of the official reserves of the sterling area in return for a $2 billion credit line. A final assurance to Pompidou in 1971 that the sterling balances would be gradually wound down was enough to placate French concerns.[27]

New Zealand's cheese and butter exports were another matter. Even though it had diversified its agricultural export outlets since the early 1960s, reducing the share going to the UK to less than two-fifths by 1970 (in 1965 Australia and New Zealand signed a free trade agreement which helped expand trade between the two countries, and bilateral security ties were strengthened after the British withdrawal east of Suez, deepening Antipodean Anglospheric relations, just as the ties to Great Britain weakened), it fought a tough rear-guard action to preserve its dairy product preferences. New Zealand's diplomatic efforts were sustained and effective, mobilising 'kith and kin' sentiment to put intense pressure on the UK government. The official Foreign Office account of the negotiations, written up by its lead negotiator, Sir Con O'Neill, went so far as to describe New Zealand as 'holding a veto over our entry to the Community' and its prime minister as 'more successful in the negotiations than anyone else'.[28] Britain would pay a stiff price for securing breathing space for New Zealand's agricultural producers, and O'Neill put an exact figure on it – £100 million more in budget contributions over five years. This was for a country that had a higher national income per head than the UK or any of the EEC Six.

Nixon's Shock Therapy

While the fate of New Zealand dairy farmers was being debated, Nixon administered his 'shock' to the global economy, unilaterally detaching the dollar from its fixed value against gold and breaking apart the fixed currency exchange rates that had anchored the Bretton Woods system. The USA had designed the Bretton Woods framework when it was a creditor country. By the 1960s it was a deficit nation, whose very success in reconstructing the post-war capitalist world economy had led to persistent trade deficits with Western Europe and Japan. It was simultaneously embarking on major rises in military and social spending under conditions of full employment and, in so doing, putting enormous pressure on the dollar. The dollar was overvalued and the international monetary system that had supported its global role could no longer be patched up through the bilateral currency swaps and gold pool arrangements that had been used in the 1960s. Efforts to repair it failed. By 1973, floating exchange rates had become entrenched, and currency fluctuations became the shock absorbers of the global economy. The sterling area finally disappeared.

The collapse of Bretton Woods inaugurated an era in which the governing frameworks of Anglo-American political economy changed profoundly. The managed international monetary system in which both the USA and the UK had a stake, as sovereigns of the world's two major currencies, was gradually replaced by a liberalised economic order under renewed American leadership. The class compromises of the post-war era, cemented on the foundations of full employment, real wage growth and the construction of the national welfare state, broke down, at first due to conflicts over coordinated wage restraint and the management of inflation, and later because of bitter struggles over the power of trade unions. At the same time, the Keynesian coordinates of macro-economic demand management and the maintenance of full employment were dismantled in favour of inflation control and public spending cuts. As the 1970s ended, Britain and the USA began the process of constructing a new neo-liberal political economy, with the financial sector at its heart.

The collapse of the Bretton Woods system also brought to a close an extended period of transition for Great Britain, the Commonwealth and her former colonies. By the early 1970s, little was left of the late Victorian doctrines that had shaped Churchill's worldview. The post-war world saw the gradual, but inexorable, diminution of economic ties with these countries, hastened in the late 1950s by currency convertibility and the rise of Western European markets. Britain had shared in the management of the Bretton Woods system, since the United States had an interest in the stability of sterling. But the UK had been eclipsed by the economic performance of the Western European economies, and also by Japan and the USA itself. The sterling area and the economic networks of the Anglo-world nations, which had been indispensable to Britain's recovery after the war, had all but disappeared by the mid-1970s. Britain had relied on loans, aid and bilateral monetary agreements from the USA to maintain her economic position. When these were cut off, as they were – to brutal effect – during the Suez crisis, Britain's relegation to the status of junior partner was all too apparent.

Britain remained a nuclear power and a permanent member of the UN Security Council, but its military 'world island' role had come to an end at the close of the 1960s, and great power status was no longer available to it. In defence, as in economics, the UK had long since ceded any claims to parity with the USA. And ties of sentiment with the empire were less powerful too. The end of the British Empire overseas had been accompanied by rising hostility, and overt racism, triggered by the arrival of Commonwealth immigrants in the UK. Notions of 'kith and kin' allegiance all too easily morphed into racial prejudice. But the tide of history was, for the most part, against such irredentism. The racial affinities that had seemed such a secure basis for Anglosphere identity before the war began to wither, both under pressure internationally, as support for racial equality, decolonisation and self-government became common diplomatic currency, and within the UK itself, as anti-racist struggles found their way into mainstream politics. These swirling currents of race, sovereignty and post-colonial anxiety would find their most explosive and toxic expression in the figure of Enoch Powell, as we shall see.

Despite residual support for the Commonwealth, Britain's turn to Europe and away from the old ties of empire was confirmed by the mid-1970s – and endorsed by a two-thirds majority in a referendum held in 1975 by the returning Wilson government as a means of papering over its internal party divisions on the issue. The Commonwealth could no longer plausibly figure as a strategic reason for staying out of Europe, despite Eurosceptic claims that it had been 'betrayed' by Britain's decision. For Julian Amery, Leo's son and heir to the Chamberlainite tradition, there was 'no valid alternative for Britain to Europe. We cannot find safety or growth on a purely national basis.

Nor can we recreate the British Commonwealth', he wrote
to Heath. 'We have to make Europe the central theme of
our policy, in much the same way as the Conservative
Party made Commonwealth and Empire its central theme
from Joe Chamberlain's time to the 1950s.'[29]

It is a commonplace to say that Britain left it too long
to make this strategic choice, passing up all the opportunities offered in the 1950s for exercising decisive influence
on the course of events in Europe. But in the immediate
post-war period Britain still depended too heavily on the
Commonwealth and colonies for its economic recovery
and political clout. Nor was Europe asking to be led, as
Milward pointed out. The judgement that engagement in
Western Europe should have been the primary focus of
British economic and foreign policy in the immediate post-
war years is too reliant on hindsight. Moving within the
circumferences of Churchill's three circles made sense to
policy-makers and remained the most viable approach
available to them.

Only when Britain's worldwide role had become an
encumbrance it could no longer afford; when the 'stop–go'
economic policies of maintaining a global reserve currency
and pre-war trade patterns had led to relative economic
decline; when the failure to invest in the modernisation of
British industry had led to weakening productivity relative
to the rest of the advanced capitalist world; and when
decolonisation and the gradual break-up of the old Anglo-
world had stripped the Commonwealth of any meaningful
political or economic unity did Britain's thinking about its
place in the world change. When it did, the country joined
the EEC on terms worse than those that might have been
achieved in the late 1950s. By then, Europe was, often
grudgingly, seen as a necessary choice. The pull of the
Anglosphere had waned considerably, but the lure of
America was still considerable for Britain's elite.

4

The Powellite Interlude: Sovereignty, Decline and the Return to England

As the 1960s progressed, the bedrock assumptions under-pinning established views of Britain's place in the world were increasingly called into question. This was in part the result of deepening worries about the UK's relatively poor economic performance, but also because new issues arose, bringing to the fore questions about the purpose and future direction of Britain. These included the future course of the Commonwealth and the question of whether Britain's future lay in the newly formed EEC. These shifts were put into dramatic relief by the conversion of Enoch Powell from a well-regarded Conservative backbencher and min-ister into an anti-establishment iconoclast. His outspoken opposition to the direction of travel taken by his own party – the Conservatives – on immigration and then the EEC – turned into an audacious attempt to stake out an alterna-tive political vision for British Conservatism.[1] The increas-ingly resonant arguments about nationality, immigration and sovereignty that he advanced looked like a sharp turn away from the kind of expansive, outward-facing and global self-image portrayed by Churchill and earlier pro-ponents of 'Greater Britain'. But, while there is undoubt-edly some truth in this characterisation, it is also important to understand the ways in which Powell reworked some of the constituent themes of Anglosphere thinking rather than rejecting them altogether. His desire to challenge established views about Britain's position in the world and its national interests put a significant dent in the 'great power complex' which Churchill had done so much to sustain. Yet a careful examination of Powell's evolving thinking reveals that the Anglosphere continued to structure important parts of his outlook and that of the growing number of nationalists and populists who have come after him.[2] The Anglosphere lived on into the era of 'after empire', but in a very different form.

The changing international context of the post-war years was a crucial spur to the anti-consensus arguments about nationhood and sovereignty which Powell began to advance. As Britain's rulers hesitated over the dilemma associated with choosing between the Commonwealth and the Anglosphere, on the one hand, and the EEC, on the other, they remained deeply dependent upon the leadership of the United States in world affairs. But, by the end of the 1960s, the consensus about the need for Britain to find a point of balance between its post-imperial and European interests, which Churchillian thinking had helped foster, was shattered, and disagreement over these options moved to the political forefront. And while references to Britain as a great power were still commonplace, this was becoming a much more difficult claim to substantiate. The Commonwealth, as we saw in chapter 3, was now increasingly depicted as a pathway to the past, a hangover from the era of imperial preference, and viewed by modernisers of both right and left as an unhelpful crutch to which Britain was still inclined to cling. And, for a growing number of political figures, joining the EEC emerged as an attractive, alternative trajectory. But others resisted such arguments and held to the integral relationship between Britain and its former colonies, especially its white settler peoples.

The deepening divisions associated with these different options coincided with growing unease in some quarters at the rising levels of immigration from the countries of the Commonwealth, particularly from Britain's African and Asian former colonies. Settled ideas about the character of the British nation were increasingly called into question. This trend too created a significant opportunity for Powell to gain a hearing and to present himself as one of the very few political figures of his generation able and willing to join the preoccupations of mainstream politics to the vernacular sentiments of ordinary people. The cornerstone of his increasingly outspoken interventions from the middle of the 1960s was the contention that imperial ambition and the delusions of great power status had allowed the country's rulers to lose touch with the values, tradition and meanings of the nation they governed. The nation was now in peril, and it was to the forgotten English heritage that Powell urged the Conservatives to return. He supplied an often poetic vision of a nation that needed to be reborn, freed from the delusions of empire. It was obvious to Powell that Britain remained a beacon and source of influence for those countries that gravitated towards the English values of free trade, parliamentary democracy and the rule of law. But notions of transnational union and fixed alliances in international relations should, he believed, be abandoned. It was time to replant the Anglosphere in English soil.

The Remaking of Powell

Powell's heterodox stance on these issues stemmed from a gradual process of disillusion and rethinking on his part, which gradually came to pass in the 1950s. He had entered Conservative Party politics as an ardent advocate of empire and in the early days of his political career flirted with the idea of imperial federation.[3] He shared the inveterate hostility to the erosion of Britain's position in the subcontinent exhibited by diehard Conservatives and famously shocked Churchill when, as a young advisor, he provided a detailed plan for the reconquest of India.[4] But its struggle for independence represented a major blow to his outlook. And, as decolonisation began, he started to view Britain's remaining imperial commitments in very different terms.

During the 1950s his views on this, and other related subjects, began to shift quite markedly. Powell was a member of the Suez Group of Tory MPs who opposed the removal of British troops from the Suez Canal. But, after British troops left in June 1956, he broke with this faction and voted against the attempt to retake the canal on the grounds that Britain could no longer plausibly act as a global power. Soon afterwards he started to gravitate towards positions that set him against the leadership of his own party, and indeed the political establishment more generally. This transformation was rooted in his deepening frustration at the hold which empire still exerted upon Britain's rulers. But this was a chapter in their history which the British needed to close. Empire was a passing phase, its enduring ethos a 'mirage', not an integral aspect of the identity of the nation. The country's rulers were suffering from a profound 'post-imperial neurosis', as a once great nation was in danger of overreaching itself while simultaneously seeking refuge under the American nuclear umbrella. A deep suspicion of American hegemony represented one of his most enduring convictions.[5]

Powell viewed the emerging Commonwealth association with suspicion from the outset. This was little more than a 'farce' or 'sham' – a meaningless confederation in which countries exhibited no allegiance to each other, and over which Britain lacked any actual authority. This stance was first publicly apparent in March 1953 in the notable speech he delivered, as a backbencher, in response to the government's Royal Titles Bill. The fading glory of empire had been transposed onto a constitutionally incoherent union, he argued, which lulled the British into believing that they still led the world.

Instead, the English should look back over the compass of their own history, including the lengthy period before empire, to start to rediscover who they were and what their national mission now should be. Appreciating England's unmatched cultural heritage and understanding the unique achievement of a system of government based upon parliamentary sovereignty were now imperative. It was England, and its exceptional lineage, that Powell came to embrace with a fervour which his predecessors had reserved for 'Greater Britain'. This national outlook undercut the ingrained habit of depicting England as a nation whose interests and outlook were expressed in entities larger than itself – empire and, latterly, the Commonwealth. But despite his critique of imperial consciousness, Powell's own conception of England's past was shot through with assumptions about past glories and greater achievements.[6] In the current era, by contrast, a combination of liberalism, the emerging idea of multiculturalism, and a lingering belief in the duties associated with empire meant that such patriotic sensibilities were somehow frowned upon or denounced for their racialist content.

English Nationalism

Powell's rhetoric grew more passionate and demotic as the 1960s progressed. And his outspoken stance on the perils of immigration towards the decade's end was soon followed by his decision to speak out against the UK's entry to the Common Market. Increasingly, he came to believe that such a model of economic union was bound to require forms of political and legal integration which would put in jeopardy Britain's unique model of parliamentary sovereignty. These contrarian standpoints stemmed from the radical rejection of the grand Churchillian vision which he began to question during the 1950s. There was an innate glory and splendour to Britain, but this did not depend upon the trappings of empire. Instead of the English being seen as the hub of a global network of imperial peoples, they were depicted as a once mighty, but increasingly overlooked, populace who needed to reaffirm and reclaim their own national culture. This meant casting to one side the imperial model of British citizenship which now threatened to reap disastrous consequences at home in the form of growing numbers of non-white immigrants to the UK.

This insistence upon the underlying durability and sense of tradition associated with Englishness stemmed from Edwardian ideas of nationhood in particular. Powell identified the principle of nationality and its close conceptual companion, sovereignty, as the key sources of allegiance binding the English people together and providing the invisible tie linking them to their unique form of government.[7] In his eyes, Englishness grew from a deep and ancient heritage and bequeathed a set of cultural habits and common practices, as well as a distinct set of political and legal institutions. A sense of belonging to a nation could be inculcated only among those steeped in the practices, customs and traditions through which it was sustained. He was, therefore, sceptical that those from 'other' national and cultural backgrounds could ever be assimilated to Englishness, and he increasingly counterposed this ancient form of nationality to the invented idea of a legalistic British citizenship. His growing sense of the divergence of these ideas set the scene for his emergence as the tribune for popular hostility to rising levels of immigration from the Commonwealth.

And so Powell set about debunking the myths that had comforted and guided the British elite since 1945. He called upon the English, no longer at the hub of an expansive empire or the workshop of the world, to see themselves in a different way – as part of a national lineage in possession of age-old virtues that needed to be brought back to the fore. He also called for the renovation of the English lineage of free market exchange, the limited state, and lives lived in stable and ordered communities. Shorn of the delusions of 'Greater Britain', the UK should limit its military ambitions to its proximate neighbourhood and operate more independently of American power. Despite his deep hostility to forms of transnational economic union, he came to believe that Britain needed to reimagine itself as a primarily European power in its reach and influence.

The controversial public positions – on immigration, Europe and Ulster – which Powell adopted in these years, and the political isolation that resulted from them, turned him into a pariah in mainstream politics.[8] And this position was solidified in the years that followed, culminating in his call for voters to support the Labour Party in the general election of 1974. Yet, despite his growing marginalisation within the party system, Powell's impact upon the wider public discourse and the Conservative wing of British politics was deep and long-lasting. This was certainly true in terms of his identification of immigration and Europe as issues that evoked deep feelings rooted in sovereignty and identity among many of the English. Powell used the terms 'England', 'Britain' and 'UK' pretty much interchangeably, signalling his deep beliefs in the unitary character of a state that was governed by the Crown-in-Parliament and the integral relationship between parliamentary government and the English inheritance. But he also 'saw England and the English as the overwhelming force within that nation'.[9] He was the first political figure in the post-war period to sense and give expression to the distinctive ways in which the English as a people felt about their state and nationhood.

This alternative vision began to take shape during the 1950s. There are a few glimpses of it in the rather conventional version of the national story – *Biography of a Nation* – which Powell jointly authored with Angus Maude in 1955.[10] But it was expressed more fully in some of the speeches he delivered from this point onwards. He believed that an English cultural background was available only to those from the same ethnic stock who had been inculcated into the common habits and forms of understanding unique to the national tradition. This, together with the quasi-spiritual manner in which he tended to

invoke Englishness, began to mark out his patriotism as
highly distinctive in character and tone. In the – subsequently iconic – St George's Day speech which he delivered
in 1961, he celebrated the enduring 'mystery of England',
its unnoticed, but very real, presence at the heart of the
British system of governance and law.[11] He proceeded to
call upon the powerful ancestral forces which lay behind
the English idea, while stoutly resisting the modern inclination to define or stipulate what Englishness was. Summon-
ing England's forebears, he asked that they 'tell us what it
is that binds us together' and 'show us the clue that leads
through a thousand years; whisper to us the secret of this
charmed life of England, that we in our time may know
how to hold it fast.'[12] Renewing and regaining the nation
were acts of faith rather than forms of rational enquiry or
cultural definition, and they required ritualistic observa-
tion and respect.

The English after empire, Powell went on, were returning home, just like the Athenians coming back to their city
to find that it had been sacked and burned. Albion was,
metaphorically, smouldering and damaged, with the conditions for its integrity challenged and its cultural heritage
facing mortal threat. Empire was now presented as a risky
journey away from the homeland of the English, and it
was the latter which – despite its ravaged and disordered
appearance – remained the true source of meaning and
security. As he put it, 'the nationhood of the mother
country remained unaltered through it all, almost uncon-
scious of the strange fantastic structure built around her';
and 'England ... underwent no organic change as the mis-
tress of a World Empire. So the continuity of her existence
was unbroken.' What also remained intact, he observed,
was 'the homogeneity of England, so profound and embracing that the counties and the regions make it a hobby to
discover their differences and assert their particularities.'

Drawing upon such elegiac and ancestral ideas, Powell
was able to present the arrival of small, but growing,
numbers of immigrants from other cultures and nations

as an existential threat to the national lineage. Those from different cultural backgrounds and traditions represented an inherent dilution of it and might well become the source of civil conflict. His dramatic shift of position on this particular issue was an important prelude to the increasingly strident calls he began to make from the mid-1960s for a change in the government's approach to immigration.[13] His increasingly apocalyptic warnings about an English identity under threat from immigration paved the way for later generations of populist rhetoric on this score. Powell talked of 'the sense of being a persecuted minority which is growing among ordinary English people in the areas of the country which are affected',[14] establishing a potent imaginative connection between new arrivals from the Commonwealth and the systematic 'persecution' of the English.

Immigration

It was his outspokenness on the immigration question, above all, that turned Powell into the apocalyptic and controversial figure he became. His sensitivity to this question, and specifically some of the legal aspects associated with it, had long been apparent. He had become exercised during the debates about the Royal Titles Bill of 1953 and spoke on other occasions in debates about the status of Commonwealth countries and their citizens. This particular piece of legislation, which gave statutory recognition to the end of empire and the demise of the 'British Commonwealth', was seen by most parliamentarians as a technical piece of legal adjustment. But to Powell it created the absurd situation whereby the monarch was now to be head of a Commonwealth over which she did not have dominion, since some of its members were now republics. Previously he had expressed strong concerns about Labour's Nationality Act of 1948, which he had opposed because it created distinct categories of British citizen – and thereby undermined the unity of British subjects under the crown throughout the empire.[15] The latter had – fatefully, in his eyes – moved away from the notion that the members of this association were all united by their shared allegiance to the sole source of sovereign authority, the Crown-in-Parliament. This attempt to divide up the sovereignty of the monarch was replicated in the new 1953 Bill. Such debates, and the profound worries they generated for him, were an important early marker of Powell's shifting thinking about empire and citizenship.

During the 1960s, the arrival of growing numbers of immigrants from Commonwealth countries brought these concerns back to the fore. Establishing at what point exactly Powell came to believe in the urgent need to reduce immigration has proved a contentious point among his interpreters.[16] He certainly shifted his stance on this specific question, having begun the decade seemingly content with his own party's position of supporting relatively low levels of immigration to Britain. By its end, he was outspokenly opposed, and depicted the effects of immigration into the UK in apocalyptic terms. This accentuated his worsening relationship with Conservative Party leader Edward Heath and resulted in his sacking from the shadow cabinet in 1968.[17] Moving into open conflict with his party, he broke ranks with the liberal tenor and tone that his party's leadership had come to employ on the immigration question. He repeatedly expressed scepticism about the anticipated numbers of new immigrants, consistently arguing that official figures underestimated the total numbers of likely arrivals and questioning policy towards family dependents. And from 1965 he began to call – though with some ambiguity – for programmes of voluntary repatriation.

His close association with this controversial subject brought Powell a huge amount of media attention and a new platform at a time when he was increasingly disenchanted with the political direction taken by Heath. He exploded into public consciousness following the 'Rivers of Blood' speech he delivered in April 1968 in Birmingham. In this, he conjured up the spectacle of a beleaguered and vulnerable indigenous populace at the mercy of an uncivilised, hostile and rapidly multiplying immigrant population. Speaking as the prophet cast out in his own land, he anticipated the 'chorus of execration' that would follow his remarks, as he predicted growing discord caused by the negligent immigration policies of the elite. It was his duty as the political representative of the ordinary Englishman to speak out on these matters.

The nature of this speech, on this most sensitive of issues, effectively rendered him a political outlaw. Even though Powell had in many respects been the consummate 'insider', having worked his way up through the ranks of the Conservative Party – despite some notable tensions generated by his own middle-class social background[18] – he subsequently broadened his critique of government policy, first on immigration and then on Europe, into a more expansive attack upon the political establishment as a whole. He focused in particular upon the combination of fatalism about British decline and *bien pensant* liberalism which prevailed among the country's leadership. And, over time, he came to adopt the rhetorical stance of the reviled outsider, ready to speak uncomfortable truths, masochistic in his relish for the opprobrium heaped upon him. In these ways Powell began to play the role of the populist leader, willing and able to promote the defence of the national homeland against the indifference and machinations of the elites.[19] Both appealing to a high-minded conception of national mythology and unafraid to dip into a coarser seam of street-level racism, he gave shape and respectability to a discourse of ethnic-majority nationalism which had been marginalised in British politics since 1945. In so doing, he prepared the way for Thatcher's later reconfiguration of the politics of British nationhood and also for the political potential of anti-immigrant sentiments, a connection which re-emerged powerfully in some of the arguments aired during the Brexit campaign of 2016.

And yet, Powell's nationalist populism had some notable limits, primarily because of his deep commitment to the ideal of parliamentary sovereignty which meant that he actively discouraged extra-parliamentary mobilisation.[20] He famously told a deputation of meat porters who marched in support of his stance on immigration to go home and write to their MPs.[21] And for some while he was uncomfortable with the focus upon holding a referendum on the UK's membership which had become a focus for many of his fellow Common Market sceptics, changing his mind on this issue only in 1972.

His 'Rivers of Blood' speech attracted an unprecedented public response and was an important moment in the rebirth of a Conservative populism as a force in British political culture. Powell received more than 100,000 letters within a week, and his stance stimulated supportive demonstrations from various trade unions.[22] A poll conducted in May of that year reported that 74 per cent of people agreed with his views – though his popularity ratings fell quickly in subsequent months. The correspondence he received reflected a mood of pessimism, especially among the working classes, about the fortunes of the nation in general and a complex stew of resentment and fear about the erosion of social benefits. As one commentator suggests, 'immigration was as much a symptom as a cause of social ills and national weakness.'[23] Powell served as a convenient hook upon which to hang a variety of frustrations and concerns.

The nationalism expressed in this correspondence was of a much more avowedly nostalgic kind than his own, devoted to the notion of 'the people's empire' and supportive of the 'kith and kin' vision of the English-speaking peoples of other parts of the Old Commonwealth – attachments for which Powell, ironically, had little sympathy. But it was what he had come to represent, as much as what he actually said, that assumed such importance. In particular, it was his capacity to speak to a palpable sense of melancholy and loss in working-class communities that ensured the resonance of his political rhetoric. He sensed that the flip-side to these deep sentiments of loss and melancholy were burgeoning feelings of grievance and anger, and he did all that he could – within the confines of his commitment to parliamentary government – to direct this mood towards the perennial targets of the populist imagination – untrustworthy elite politicians and undesirable aliens arriving on the homeland's shores.

Melancholy, loss and decline melded powerfully with notions of redemption, emancipation and renewal in Powell's speeches during this period. In political terms, the brand of parliamentary populism that he developed created a space that would be explored at a later point, in different ways, first by Margaret Thatcher and subsequently by proponents of Brexit.

The Politics of British Nationality

Immigration was not the only issue on which Powell was outspoken at this point in his career. The implications of the UK's potential membership of the Common Market became another major focus for his energies. As with empire and immigration, Powell's stance on this issue shifted markedly in the early 1960s. Having initially been in favour of the UK's entry, on the grounds that a European Customs Union would promote the cause of free trade, he came to denounce such a scenario, since it would necessitate forms of political and legal coordination which would invariably impinge upon national sovereignty. Rather typically, he moved towards this position via the very particular constitutional question of whether parliament could legitimately consent to constrain its own will by ceding powers to a supranational body.

Powell's acerbic hostility to European membership also placed him outside the Conservative mainstream. For many years this was a lonely field to plough on the political right, bringing him into cooperation with figures from the

left – notably Tony Benn during the referendum campaign
of 1975.[24] Indeed, it was not until the debates on the single
currency and Maastricht Treaty in the late 1980s and early
1990s that his views began to gain traction with a small
cohort of Conservatives. Many of the notes he struck
during these years of opposition were echoed by a later
generation of sceptics, especially his repeated mockery of
Brussels 'bureaucrats' and denunciation of what he saw as
vested interests at work lobbying for the European cause
– the Confederation of British Industry above all.

Powell was convinced from an early stage that Europe, as
well as immigration, would one day become a site towards
which a wider sense of resentment would be drawn:

> British membership of the Community will not stick.
> Lacking the essential foundation in opinion, it is built on
> sand. Every common policy, or attempted common policy,
> of the Community will encounter a political resentment
> in Britain ... These resentments will intertwine themselves
> with all the raw issues of British politics: inflation, unem-
> ployment, balance of payments, the regions, even immigra-
> tion, even Northern Ireland; and every one of these issues
> will be sharpened to the discomfiture of the European
> party.[25]

He was also, rather notably, opposed to membership of
the European Community because of American support
for this option. A European bloc, he believed, was destined
to be a subordinate part of a larger US-dominated Western
alliance. His own response to this issue reflected a growing
unease on parts of the political right, mirrored on the
further shores of the British left, about American influence
in Europe. And his maverick stance extended also to his
thinking about Britain's defence and security, including his
opposition to the nuclear deterrent and scepticism about
NATO. For Powell, slavish adherence to the international
alliances forged by Churchill reflected a deep-seated British
inferiority complex, and this was in turn the unwelcome
by-product of its great power delusion.

By the early 1970s Powell was an established political heretic, firmly established in the public eye as the politician ready to speak out on issues where British sovereignty and national identity were at stake. His own rhetoric became increasingly embittered in relation to Heath in particular, whom he accused of breaking his promise to secure 'the consent of the British Parliament and people' before committing to entering the new EEC. While Heath succeeded in ensuring that the UK did join, Powell gave legitimacy and impetus to the rival contention – which came back into public discourse in the run-up to Brexit – that British accession to the Common Market was an act of betrayal by a cadre of establishment politicians who had lost faith in the historical lineage and unique cultural tradition of England.

One further issue became increasingly salient in Powell's thinking during the 1970s. This concerned the position and governance of Northern Ireland in a period of growing military conflict, during a period when the British government was seeking to develop a more stable constitutional settlement for the six counties. On this issue he achieved little popular resonance in England, although he did become an influential force within the North's Unionist politics. In 1987, he denounced the Anglo-Irish Agreement signed by his one-time protégée Margaret Thatcher in embittered, personal terms.

More generally, his interventions on this issue reveal much about Powell's conception of the British state and the anti-federal nature of his thinking about the UK. Having finally decided to leave the Conservative Party, he joined the Official Unionist Party in 1974 and represented the constituency of South Down until 1987. His unfailing belief that Northern Ireland needed to be reintegrated into the UK put him at odds with most of his Unionist colleagues, and with public opinion more generally. But Powell was insistent that the people of Ulster needed to be protected not only from Republican paramilitary violence but also from the unwillingness of their own state to recognise the priority of the principles of nationality and indivisible sovereignty. What for most politicians looked like a 'law and order' question was in his mind a conflict that dramatised wider issues of sovereignty and citizenship in the UK. Speaking in 1974, he declared that this struggle 'is about nationality; and unless it is understood to be about nationality all discussion and contrivance and policy remain in the limbo of unreality and insecurity.'[26] The tendency among the UK's politicians, and the British state, to view and treat Northern Ireland as quintessentially different from other parts of the kingdom represented a fundamental breach in the compact between people and state. This was an issue that should be of concern to all British citizens and politicians.

These ideas prepared the ground for Powell's own deeply hostile response to the emergence of arguments for the devolution of powers to Scotland, and potentially Wales, during the 1970s. Parliament, he believed, was the cornerstone of the English constitutional tradition and the site where the indivisible sovereignty of the people was exercised. He therefore rejected schemes for devolution as constitutionally illegitimate attempts to devolve the indivisible sovereignty of Britain's parliamentary government.

The Anglosphere Reborn?

Powell's thinking on these various issues rested upon a coherent and distinctive understanding of Britain's history and the nature of its peoples' shared national identity. And this led him to think about a range of issues outside the parameters of Churchillian thinking and to detach from the discourse of 'Greater Britain' as articulated by Seeley. And yet, it is not entirely accurate to say that, in shifting from these traditions, Powell represented the simple negation of the ethos and ideals of the Anglosphere. In fact, he reworked parts of this lineage and in some respects sustained an older lineage of nationalist sentiment, even as he forcefully argued that the national spirit needed to be shored up and defended most powerfully at home. In this sense, he played a key role in relation to the Anglosphere concept: de-linking it from empire while leaning heavily still upon imperial ways of thinking, renewing an older tradition of Conservative nationalism, and preparing the way for the 'neo-liberal' reincarnation of this idea at the very end of the twentieth century.

Powell himself served in India from 1943 until 1946 and retained a deep interest in, and abiding affection for, the subcontinent.[27] Even as he sought to bury empire in his polemical interventions of the 1960s, it is not hard to discern a lingering nostalgia for it in his thought. In 1959, he spoke from the backbenches against racial abuses in the empire and famously denounced the treatment of Mau Mau prisoners by the British authorities in Kenya out of an enduring sense of imperial responsibility. And his account of the history and essence of England overlapped substantially with the story told by Seeley and his fellow Victorian imperialists. He too saw England as an exceptional polity which was outward-facing in its pursuit of free trade and international alliances. Indeed, the imperial past was still assumed to be an integral influence within the history and outlook of the English nation. Powell's extensive knowledge of classical sources endowed him with an inclination to conceive of the national past in cyclical rather than linear terms. The return to the English homeland which he urged upon Britain's rulers was of a piece with the previous era of expansion and civilisational leadership, not a simple negation of it. Only thus could England find its strengths and return to the habits and policies which had placed it on the road to greatness in the first place.

Powell's anti-imperialist position after 1945 reflected the belief that the ethos and outlook of one era might become weaknesses or constraints if retained in another. Empire was over, but the outward-facing and global self-image portrayed by latter-day proponents of 'Greater Britain', which still prevailed, was now over-extending the British financially and militarily. The English-speaking people of Powell's imagination were no longer the hub of a global network of settler peoples, as envisaged by Churchill, but an overlooked and increasingly resentful nation whose cultural traditions and interests were being dangerously neglected by their own state. The hangover of the imperial outlook obscured the need for a realistic and proportionate understanding of Britain's influence and place in the world. The UK was a medium-sized power with a successful economy, which needed to put aside delusions about its ability to shape events in far-flung places and focus instead upon its own regional position.[28]

In order to rescue the English from their rulers' weaknesses of mind, it was time for the Anglosphere to come home. This represented less the negation of empire and its attendant outlook and more the reflection of a classically trained appreciation of the inevitable decline and fall of empires.[29] Powell was also an increasingly pessimistic observer of those Anglophone states, notably the USA, that were attempting to devise a multicultural form of nationality. Any such venture was bound to lead to deep civil discord and was doomed to failure. Britain, by contrast, needed to throw off the two prevalent habits – of either clinging on to empire when its time was passed or seeing its own identity as one defined by the crisis of imperial dissolution.

Instead, Powell promoted the idea of English nationhood as a rich and deeply rooted lineage and the contention that this was increasingly being overlooked by the moral and political guardians of the state. In 1968 he evoked 'the sense of being a persecuted minority which is growing among ordinary English people'.[30] His depiction of a nationality that was fundamentally at odds with political discourse and state policy has cast a long shadow over British politics, and indeed over later political attempts to mould British nationhood and develop a progressive English patriotism. This post-colonial nationalism reflected a search for certainty at a point when empire was over,

and when its associated attachments and forms of imagined community seemed increasingly bereft of meaning.[31]
The quest for the reassurance of national foundations had
a neurotic feel to it and heightened and legitimated feelings
of hostility to incomers in a way that laid the foundations
for a powerful new pattern of popular racism. By the
1970s, the name 'Enoch' became synonymous with street-
level xenophobia rather than high-minded appeals to
nationality.[32]

Conclusions

Powell's heterodox politics and critique of 'Greater Britain'
can be seen as the first indication of a turning of the tide
against lingering dreams of empire in the English national
consciousness. Nevertheless, his historical and political
imagination was still infused with the assumptions and
ethos of the Anglosphere. These were now reworked for
an era of national crisis and discord, and they were applied
to England in a more concrete and bounded sense. In
Powell's mind, a post-colonial Britain shorn of fantasies
about its role at the helm of grand international alliances
was far better placed to resume the national trajectory and
economic path which had sustained its pre-eminence
during the nineteenth century. Freed from such illusions,
Britain could still play a constructive and beneficial role in
international affairs, promoting freer trade and providing
a beacon for those starting on their own journeys to
national independence. Having been compelled to give up
the colonies, the political elite needed to return to the
governance of the internal empire and its increasingly
imperilled core institutions – crown, parliament and union.

Despite Powell's own exile from mainstream politics, his
ideas – on immigration and Europe – created a space which
later demagogues and populists would come to occupy.
The demotic and populist vision of the nation which he
developed, in combination with his traditionalist Tory

understanding of the parliamentary state, combined to underpin a very different version of the Anglosphere to that associated with Churchillian hubris or Commonwealth liberalism. And this new outlook offered an important opening to cultural sources which had gone untapped in British politics since 1945 – vernacular racism, deep anti-Americanism and a sharper edged nationalism. From this period onwards, the notion of England as the host of a tradition that found expression in entities larger than itself now faced a major political and intellectual challenge, and this counter-trend was to lead, after many subsequent twists and turns, to Brexit.[33]

5

The Anglosphere in the Late Twentieth Century: Retreat and Thatcherite Reinvention

The referendum to ratify the UK's membership of the EEC held in 1975 defused the European question in British politics, but for a brief period only. This issue gradually turned into what Powell had always said it was: an increasingly sensitive site for worries about national sovereignty and identity and a source of significant division within high politics. The European question came to play an integral role in the Thatcher premierships, contributing to both her downfall and that of her successor, John Major. Thatcher's approach to the management of the UK's relationship with the EEC evolved in unpredictable ways in this period as she shifted her outlook towards the prospect of deeper economic and political integration. Her concern about whether British interests could successfully be protected within this deepening union created and reflected growing doubts within her own party about the UK's long-term relationship with Europe. And, as she moved by the end of her premiership towards a position of outright hostility to the EU, she created space for the re-emergence of older ideas about the Anglosphere which were increasingly framed as a pathway to redemption from the European venture.

During her time in office it was Anglo-America that assumed particular importance for Thatcher. Under her influence, relations with the United States were more intimate than previously, ensuring greater leverage and prestige on the international stage for the UK. The more full-throated Atlanticism to which she became committed was both ideological and strategic in character as she sought to revive the idea of a uniquely Anglo-American approach to markets, politics and statecraft.[1] As she turned emphatically in this direction, she began to pull the Conservative Party away from the European moorings associated with its previous leadership.

Early Days and Emerging Priorities

While Thatcher's main domestic priorities, especially in terms of economic and social policy, were fairly clear when she was elected, what her victory meant in terms of foreign policy was not. This was a less developed part of her own thinking and an area where she had little previous experience. While, like most Conservatives, she was in favour of the UK's membership of the EEC, her support for it was contingent upon the assumption that it represented a clear benefit to Britain's trading position and economic health. Such hopes were somewhat shaken – for her and others – by the events of 1976. The major economic crisis of that year, which culminated in the humiliating prospect of a UK government seeking a bailout from the International Monetary Fund, dented confidence in the merits of the EEC within the UK. Its limitations as a policy actor in the face of worldwide recession were laid bare, and doubts about the idea that European membership would provide an answer to the UK's economic weaknesses gained ground. At the same time, in domestic terms, this crisis dented Labour's credibility and created an opening for Thatcher to project the case for a more radical approach to fiscal and economic policy.[2]

In terms of foreign affairs, Thatcher's arrival in office seemed likely to herald a slight tilt away from the avowed Atlanticism pursued by her Labour predecessors, Wilson and Callaghan, towards the more pro-European stance associated with the Conservatives. In fact, over time, she picked up Callaghan's mantle, pursued a deeper and more ideological vision of Anglo-American alliance, and positioned the UK as guide and supporter for the USA in its role as leader of the Western alliance against the Soviet-led Eastern bloc. This approach took some while to emerge and was aided considerably by the election of Republican Ronald Reagan as president in 1980. When it did become prominent, it created some notable political risks as well as generating various opportunities and advantages for Thatcher's government.

It was also widely assumed that her election would result in a closer relationship with the countries of the 'Old Commonwealth' with which the Conservative Party had maintained close relations. Given the major political challenges arising to the rule of white settler minorities in both South Africa and Rhodesia in the 1970s, managing these issues – while retaining the goodwill of the wider Commonwealth – was bound to be difficult. The shadow of empire still hung over the UK, and for a short while this became an issue of major political and military focus following the attempt by the Argentinian government to test Britain's readiness to defend one of its most far-flung historic commitments – the Falkland Islands. Thatcher's decision to meet this challenge by assembling a military force was seen by some critics as a symptom of the neo-imperial fantasy associated with her vision of 'putting the Great back into Great Britain'.[3] In fact, her thinking on this issue was driven mainly by domestic political considerations, as well as by an intuitive sense of the symbolism associated with it.[4] Towards the end of her time in office, another imperial issue arose in relation to the position of the former British colony Hong Kong, which was due to revert to Chinese control in 1997. Her pragmatic handling of these negotiations did not indicate any deep-seated desire to fight imperial battles for the sake of it.

Thatcher retained a strong sense of herself as a figure emanating from the English provinces, a relative outsider to a political establishment that was in key respects more collectivist in its thinking than she was. The sense of strength she drew from her English identity, and her growing willingness to frame the Conservatives as radical opponents of public institutions and bodies, pulled her towards the political space which Powell had opened.[5] As her own relations with other European leaders deteriorated and her wariness towards the prospect and implications of integration grew, she came to occupy this niche more resolutely and boldly – and indeed won Powell's approval for the stance she took on the European question after 1987.

Anglo-America

Thatcher's own foreign policy thinking was ultimately anchored in her unshakeable conviction that the most fundamental threat facing the Western order emanated from communism in general and Soviet aggression in particular. In the face of the alliance headed by the USSR, she promoted the idea of a tight-knit Western alliance with the USA at its helm, a strong NATO and the retention of an effective nuclear deterrent. Her view of the Cold War between the totalitarian East and the freedom-loving West had an epic dimension to it. As she put it in a speech delivered after her time in office:

> The Cold War was not just about military power and the threat of nuclear holocaust. At its deepest level, at its most important level, it was a battle of ideas, a clash of ideologies each rooted in different conceptions of the state and the nature of man ... The great intellectual struggle must continue until democracy and freedom triumph.[6]

Throughout her premiership she invested heavily in her own image as resolute defender of the West against the USSR and its allies, and this undoubtedly helped her become an influential, if also divisive, world leader. More importantly still, it served an important purpose domestically, enabling her to present her Labour opponents as stranded on the wrong side of a profound divide. It also helped her draw attention to the party's struggles to shift away from the iconic policy that was favoured by many of its activists and MPs but was unpopular among the wider electorate – unilateral nuclear disarmament.

But the close relationship with the United States which this stance implied was never entirely easy, and some notable tensions and disagreements relating to it arose. A particular challenge was to present the special relationship as a bulwark for British sovereignty, not a source of its erosion, a prospect that could easily reawaken memories of Suez. When in 1983 the USA led an invasion of the small Caribbean island of Grenada, a former British colony, without informing the British beforehand, Thatcher was lukewarm in her public support and incandescent in private.[7] Her fear was that the British might appear subordinate or irrelevant to the pursuit of American interests. And, for the successful prosecution of the Falklands conflict in 1982, the logistical and intelligence assistance provided by the USA were key but were not immediately forthcoming, as Secretary of State Alexander Haig sought to broker a diplomatic solution between the two countries. The wary approach of the American political establishment to Britain's appeal for support offered an uncanny echo of the tensions which Churchill had been required to manage during the Second World War.[8]

In military terms, the purchase of the Trident weapons system from the United States in 1982 and the lack of British jurisdiction over American bases where nuclear weapons and military personnel were stationed were sources of concern to many Conservatives as well as Thatcher's left-wing opponents. The ingrained tendency for the USA to make major geo-political and military decisions without consulting its closest allies – as for instance over the ill-fated Star Wars Defence programme – offered uncomfortable reminders that the special relationship could mean subordination, rather than elevation, for Britain.

Towards the end of Thatcher's time in office, a much deeper fault line in the UK's relationship with the USA opened up following the dramatic collapse of the communist regimes of Eastern Europe and the onset of a new debate about the geo-political future of Europe. Thatcher's Atlanticism was exposed by this development, as the senior partner in the relationship accepted the case for extending the EEC and reunifying Germany.[9] This prospect unnerved Thatcher and some senior members of her cabinet and cut across the doctrine of the balance of power which she, and her predecessors in British government, had employed to inform the UK's strategy towards Europe. By 1989 she was convinced that schemes for political union in Europe were a ratchet that was turning in ways that Britain could not feasibly control and which would ultimately play into the hands of those, most notably the French, who wanted Europe to become a military and economic bloc to rival the USA.

The Commonwealth

It was not just in relation to the United States, however, that Thatcher brought a distinctive approach to bear upon the UK's foreign policy. This was also true of the Commonwealth. Whereas Wilson and Callaghan had identified the UK with the liberal doctrine of racial equality and a broadly consensual approach to the management of this loose association, Thatcher's early dealings with the African challenges she faced signalled a significant shift of tenor and approach. On her arrival in office she inherited an ongoing crisis in Rhodesia, resulting from the attempt of an irredentist white minority to hold on to power and the emergence of a nationalist party of opposition supported by the majority of black citizens. The broad thrust of UK policy, established since the early 1960s, had been to support the gradual transition to stable democratic rule while doing all that was feasible to offset the prospect of the emergence of anti-British forces in former colonial countries.[10]

The specific issue to which Thatcher was soon compelled to respond was the demand, supported by most Commonwealth countries, that the UK continue to impose sanctions upon the Smith regime. Her own instinct – on this question and other situations during her tenure – was to avoid sanctions, while trying to exert informal pressure upon the white settler leadership to adopt a more pragmatic line. Initially she was persuaded by her experienced foreign secretary, Lord Carrington, and the Foreign and Commonwealth Office to accept the credentials of the moderate party led by Abel Muzorewa. Throughout the subsequent negotiations with the various parties, she proved unwilling to bend to the demands of the Commonwealth. Carrington's skilful brokering of negotiations over a new constitution for Rhodesia and arrangements for a peaceful transition paved the way for elections. To Britain's consternation, however, these resulted in the victory of the radical wing of the Patriotic Front, led by Robert Mugabe. The newly created state of Zimbabwe was declared independent in April 1980.[11]

The difficult political legacy of this settlement helped convince Thatcher that the FCO was one of a number of state institutions which were neither able nor willing to promote British interests with enough assertiveness. And a gap opened between her and her foreign secretary on various other issues – most notably on the question of the UK's political role within the EEC and its stance towards the Middle East, where Thatcher favoured a more stoutly pro-Israeli line than he did. His resignation, following the sudden outbreak of the war with Argentina in 1982, provided an important opportunity for her to exercise a more direct influence over British foreign policy as a whole, and its approach to Europe in particular.[12] Thatcher's willingness to invest politically, as well as militarily, in the high-stakes expedition to retake the Falkland Islands in 1982 – against the initial advice of some senior military and political figures – bolstered her own government's weakening political position and enabled her to appropriate the themes of patriotism and British renewal to telling political effect.

The Falklands conflict was a direct hangover of empire, as this former colony remained under British jurisdiction at the behest of a majority of its English-speaking inhabitants, and Thatcher, like most of the political establishment, believed that its loss would represent a significant dent to British authority abroad. But in political terms the motivation behind it was primarily domestic, and the sending of the task force to the South Atlantic did not herald any wider interest, on Thatcher's part, in breathing new life into post-imperial politics, including the Commonwealth. Throughout her time in office, a vociferous minority of backbench MPs hoped that she would respond to their calls for a more openly supportive policy, along 'kith and kin' lines, in relation to Rhodesia and South Africa. The latter had now become a pariah state throughout the world. Thatcher did on occasions give succour to these kinds of sentiment, taking a stand against calls to boycott South Africa and repeatedly making the case for moderate and incremental change as the regime began to buckle under economic and diplomatic pressure. In her mind this was more of a Cold War than a post-colonial issue. South Africa was part of the West, while she was wary of the main political opposition, the African National Congress, and its communist affiliations. Her unwillingness to move with the direction of majority international opinion on this question placed considerable strain on the UK's relationship with other parts of the Commonwealth.

By the time Thatcher resigned, in 1990, the Commonwealth link was no longer viewed as a bulwark for British influence. This was in part a reflection of its declining importance for Britain in these years but also on account of its eclipse by the Anglo-American alliance during her premiership. As one leading historian concludes, 'She had little time for the Commonwealth, and least of all for its African leaders.'[13] And yet, while this was no longer one of the 'circles' integral to Britain's place in the world, the older idea of the UK renewing its unique relations with the countries of the 'white dominions' did, during these years, begin to re-emerge at the political margins and was given new life mainly because of the turn against Europe which Thatcher engendered among some British Conservatives.

Europe

It was in her dealings with Britain's partners in Europe, above all, that Thatcher began to exercise her most decisive and enduring impact upon the UK's foreign policy. Having started her premiership as an undoctrinaire supporter of the UK's membership, she finished in a position of open conflict with the architects of a changing Europe. Her shifting position over the years on this question was an important dynamic that helped trigger a major reversal of outlook within the two main political parties.[14] Having started the decade as the most anti-European party in British politics, her Labour opponents finished it as more pro-Europe than the Tories, in part because Thatcher's domestic domination made the idea of 'social Europe', advanced by Commission President (from 1985) Jacques Delors, more appealing to party and trade unions. The Conservatives ended up moving in the opposite direction – embarking, at Thatcher's behest, after 1988, on a crusade against political union in Europe. This was also the period in which a push towards closer integration was favoured by all of the leading states within the Community, except the UK. The Thatcher government was notably ambivalent on this score, favouring arrangements that would reduce obstacles to free trade but wary of moves towards forms of economic and political union that might impinge upon national sovereignty. This issue gradually became a major source of disagreement among British Conservatives, serving to splinter the Thatcherite camp as different figures and groups within its compass came to favour different institutional solutions to the dilemmas posed by demands for further economic integration.

The Callaghan administration's reluctance to engage with emerging arguments for greater economic and political union in the EEC, and its decision not to put the pound into the newly formed European Monetary System (EMS) in 1978, formed an important prelude to the Thatcher period. She had herself supported sterling's entry into the EMS at this point, but she was soon thrown into a difficult set of negotiations over the European budget and the size of the rebate that the UK was owed within it. Britain was one of the largest net contributors to the EEC, but some of the key programmes which the Community supported, such as the Common Agricultural Policy, were of little direct benefit to Britain because of the size of its industrial sectors and its history of importing food. Thatcher pursued the goal of securing a 'just' rebate for Britain in an uncompromising fashion, acutely aware that, in straightened economic circumstances, voters at home were watching carefully for signs that their first female prime minister might not be holding her own in these negotiations. Her uncompromising approach, and the nationalist rhetoric in which she bathed the outcome of these dealings, irked some of her fellow leaders and flouted the informal norms associated with the Community's internal operations. The deal which Thatcher eventually secured, in 1984 at the Fontainebleau summit, was hailed as a success by the British press, but it positioned Britain as an isolated player on key issues and drew the French and Germans into a closer alliance.[15]

Thatcher resumed her belligerent manner during the negotiations leading up to the watershed Single European

Act of 1986, while also showing greater adroitness than in her previous dealings with her Community partners.[16] But, to pursue her favoured cause of freer trade, she was required to accept a linkage (whether wittingly or not remains the subject of some debate)[17] between these free market rules, on the one hand, and the awarding of new powers to the European Commission and the commitment to pursue talks aimed at political integration, on the other. The Act set in train a further round of negotiations and summits which focused in more detail on monetary union, as well as on measures for deeper political and legal integration. Thatcher's leading role in creating this keynote agreement, which many 'Thatcherites' later denounced, remains the source of considerable controversy.[18] The Act introduced majority voting into the Council of Ministers and resulted in the pooling of more sovereignty than any other passed since 1972.

Thatcher's unease at the mixed outcome of these negotiations soon turned into open opposition as a powerful new connection emerged in European political discourse – between the argument for further political integration and support for more substantive social provision and regulation in areas such as employment rights. The championing of both of these agendas by the Commission president, Jacques Delors, quickly established him as a new public enemy against whom Thatcher was quick to define her own position. But leading members of her political circle were now divided on what was the best response to the integration agenda. Senior figures such as Geoffrey Howe lined up behind a growing chorus of voices in the City of London who favoured taking steps to develop a single currency, on the grounds that this was an important mechanism in the development of free market Europe. Others, including Thatcher herself, saw in this scheme an unacceptable impediment to the fiscal autonomy of states, and she increasingly came to place the goal of sovereignty over liberal economics in this theatre.

From 1987 onwards, Thatcher was embroiled in arguments about Europe that cut deeply into her own party and cabinet and threatened to exacerbate other factional differences. Her own preference for EMS over the European Exchange Rate Mechanism (ERM), and the extent of support for the latter option among other senior Tories, emerged as the source of a deepening cleavage within her cabinet. Lawson, her chancellor, viewed linking the pound to the Deutschmark as the best means of pursuing the core Thatcherite goal of lowering inflation. He and Howe forced the prime minister to fall behind this position at the Madrid summit of 1989, using their potential resignations as a powerful point of leverage. But Thatcher was not deterred and instigated the production of alternative plans for a form of currency integration congruent with her preferred model of a free market union, culminating in the development of its short-lived proposal for a hard ECU.[19]

By this point in Thatcher's premiership, Europe was both a contributor to and a barometer of a deepening divide within the ranks of the parliamentary Conservative Party. The first stirrings of the divisions this would generate had been felt in 1986. At that point she faced the most significant revolt of her premiership, on a matter relating to Britain's orientation to Europe and the USA. It stemmed from the dramatic resignation of her rising political rival Michael Heseltine, following an intense debate within government about whether a failing military manufacturer should be bailed out by an American company or rescued by a European consortium (his preferred option). Thatcher's preference for the other outcome signalled the extent to which her free market principles were now intertwined with her Anglo-American view of world order. But Europe was increasingly becoming a difficult theatre in which to project this relationship.

These tensions were accentuated by the collapse of communism towards the end of the decade – the overbearing enemy against which Thatcher had helped define the West – and by the growing likelihood that East and

West Germany would come together, creating an economic and political powerhouse in central Europe.[20] In 1988 she delivered a controversial speech in Bruges in which she appeared to offer the most principled objection to European integration that had come from a British premier since the UK had joined the EEC back in 1973. This shift was in truth more tonal than substantive, but it left the indelible impression that the UK was fundamentally opposed to the integration agenda and to the prospect of 'social Europe.'[21] Thatcher's address drew the notable approval of Powell, who applauded her insistence upon the bedrock principle of national sovereignty. She also proposed a looser union as an alternative pathway to that currently being pursued. The project for European political union, she declared, was the result of rationalistic design and represented the kind of dangerously utopian project dreamed up by intellectuals. It was increasingly the opposite to the kind of union that any authentic Conservative could support. The speech also set out more fully an alternative free market model for Europe. It provided the language and ideas that became the template for an emerging wave of Euroscepticism in British politics.

More immediately, it was followed by Thatcher's public opposition to the Maastricht Treaty, which was ratified in 1993. Her successor (from 1990), John Major, while sharing much of her outlook on Europe, reverted to the more consensual and cautious approach from which she had increasingly departed. Having wrung a number of key concessions from his partners, including the right to opt out of the proposed Social Chapter, he proceeded to take this agreement (the so-called Maastricht Bill) through parliament in 1992–3. This provided the occasion for a coordinated set of backbench revolts from within the Tory Party, leaving him able to progress only with the support of other parties in Westminster, a process which significantly weakened the standing of his party and government. Europe was now a major source of political division and policy uncertainty on the right of British politics. The

Conservative government's decision to join the ERM in late 1990 helped trigger both economic and political crises as increasingly desperate attempts to raise interest rates to keep the pound above the agreed lower limit stipulated by this mechanism failed to work, leaving sterling weak and vulnerable to speculation. The UK crashed out of the ERM on 16 September 1992 – on what came to be known as 'Black Wednesday' – an event that further emboldened opponents of the European enterprise and raised questions about the party's economic competence among key groups of voters.[22]

Thatcher's decision, after leaving office, to accept an invitation to serve as chair of the newly formed Bruges Group of Eurosceptic MPs represented the culmination of an unpredictable, but fateful, journey in her thinking about Britain's place in Europe. Despite her own initial support for her party's policy on this issue, and her role as one of the architects of the Single European Act, her main political legacy in this area was to create the impetus for a more full-throated scepticism towards European integration to take root in the UK party system. This position sowed some of the seeds that were harvested in the later campaign for Brexit. With some irony, Thatcher played an important role in the subsequent destruction of one of the three central pillars which her great hero, Churchill, believed to be fundamental to British influence.

Evaluating Thatcher

For some Conservatives, Thatcher became the first political martyr in the Eurosceptic cause.[23] To her detractors, she isolated Britain during a key period in the development of the EU, pushed France together with Germany in opposition to the UK, and diminished the ability of British policy-makers to exercise much of an influence upon the reconfiguration of Europe after 1989.[24] But neither of these polarised judgements offers a sufficiently nuanced picture of her evolving geo-political ambitions and the approach she adopted on different issues relating to international politics in this period.

Her pronounced hostility to the pessimism and fatalism which she believed were rampant in elite circles undergirded Thatcher's belief that greater assertiveness in policy terms was the best response to worries about the UK's economic position and diminished international standing. She effected a break from the governing framework of British foreign policy since the 1960s, as she placed the UK in fundamental tension with other leading powers in Europe, accentuated a deepening cleavage with the Commonwealth, and tethered British interests to US leadership of the Western alliance.[25] By 1990, the overlapping circles at the heart of Churchill's thinking were further apart from each other than at any point since 1945.

Few who witnessed her rise would have predicted that Thatcher would become a transformational prime minister, least of all in the realm of foreign affairs. In 1973, according to a report in her local newspaper, the *Finchley Times*, she presented herself as the scourge of those 'isolationists' in her own party who did not grasp the changing realities of the UK's place in the world and the abiding importance for Britain of joining the EEC.[26] This was the realistic option, she declared, because of the inclination of the leading core of 'inner' Commonwealth states – notably Australia and Canada – to turn away from Britain and develop closer trading and political links with their neighbours. The Commonwealth was fading and Europe was rising, and there was no question, she and many Conservatives believed, that the latter was the theatre where Britain's role as a great power could be sustained. An ingrained isolationism in British foreign policy, she was reported as saying, needed to be replaced by a more outward outlook, including closer engagement with Europe. In support of this stance she turned to Churchill for support: 'The great visionary of politics, Winston Churchill, had the idea to draw Europe together with a unity of voice and action.'

Two decades later, it was the very prospect of a 'common European voice' and a deeper pooling of sovereignty that drove her to break with Churchill's dictum.

This happened to a considerable extent because of changing circumstances as much as the exercise of Thatcher's own political will. Indeed, her complex and shifting position on Europe was affected more by situational factors than her advocates and critics often suggest. Two particularly important unanticipated changes in this respect were, first, the growing political will among leading European states for deeper integration than was anticipated by the Community's founders and, second, the demise of communism and its unpredictable effects on European politics.[27] At the same time, diminishing confidence in the economic and social policies pursued in the decades after 1945 created an opening for the revival of older arguments about the merits of freer markets, and these were particularly influential in some of the countries of the Anglosphere, notably the USA, the UK and New Zealand. For Thatcher, this created a welcome opportunity to frame an identity and sense of purpose around Anglo-America that went beyond questions of diplomacy and foreign policy. Indeed, a notable part of her legacy was the legitimacy she accorded to the lingering idea that Britain's real identity lay not in Europe but in its historical allegiance with other English-speaking peoples. Thatcher herself was not noticeably interested in the wider Anglosphere until she left office, when she delivered several notable addresses on the common heritage and future importance of the English-speaking peoples.[28] But she bequeathed to those interested in this idea the conviction that membership of the EU might be an interlude – not the terminus – for Britain and a powerful body of rhetoric about the English origins of Western ideals such as self-government, the rule of law and free markets.

For a small band of Conservatives, in the UK and other English-speaking countries, this was an increasingly appealing vision in a context where European economies appeared to be stalling and new engines of growth were emerging in the Eastern hemisphere. Some took to arguing that the UK needed to reject the model of social Europe and reinvent itself as the Hong Kong of Europe – a deregulated, low-tax and flexible economy, with trading relationships across the world. And increasingly these dreams, which were fired by Thatcher's turn away from the European mainstream, began to take hold on parts of the political right.

The New Right Anglosphere

In the years following Thatcher's departure from office, politics in Anglo-America took a very different turn. The election of Democrat President Bill Clinton in 1992 and Tony Blair's accession to office after his landslide victory in 1997 seemed to represent the demise of neo-liberal Atlanticism and its replacement by a new, centrist Anglo-American political alliance. During the late 1990s and early 2000s, European integration gathered pace, a raft of new countries in Eastern Europe were admitted to the EU, and new kinds of international cooperation were promoted and explored. Blair returned to an older model of statecraft, pitching the UK as the conduit between Europe and America, and engaged more deeply in European policy debates. Anglo-American cooperation returned to the fore as Clinton and Blair collaborated closely in relation to various international crises, most notably Kosovo. And there were echoes of the Reagan–Thatcher era as they reprised the idea of a shared ideological vision, this time based upon their commitment to a combination of free markets and greater social investment. And, in this context, the ideas and positions associated with the Thatcherite right were consigned to the political margins.

At this point, dreams of the Anglosphere went into near abeyance in British politics, and a broadly liberal, pro-European internationalism emerged as a natural companion to New Labour's ascendancy. But it was out of the experience of forced exile that this older lineage was to be reborn. It was incubated, nurtured and reconfigured during the late 1990s and early 2000s by a small but influential transatlantic network of entrepreneurs, pundits, intellectuals, media moguls and maverick politicians. This was a community forged around shared ideas and aspirations but which lacked a wider social constituency, a political vehicle and – until a few years later – mainstream exponents. Yet it was in these years that the Anglosphere ideal was powerfully reinvented for the changing conditions associated with the advent of the twenty-first century.

The Anglosphere concept was now reframed in relation to debates about globalisation, and its ties to the imperial past were quite significantly loosened, if not entirely expunged. And, now, Churchill's third circle – Europe – was increasingly depicted as the major constraint upon the realisation of the dream of reunifying the English-speaking peoples. Britain, it was increasingly suggested, needed to turn away from continental Europe and find its way back to the open sea. A small community was brought together to share these ideas at a sequence of high-level conferences and symposiums and by a number of neo-conservative institutes. The prospects for a new alignment between the English-speaking nations became the abiding focus of this network, but this old thesis was now reinvented in the context of contemporary debates about American decline, the rise of China and the emergence of a new, potentially existential, threat to Western order in the shape of Islamic radicalism, as we shall explore in the next chapter.

The full story of the emergence of this New Right Anglosphere is yet to be told, primarily because the identity of its main donors and the nature of the relationships between its key figures remain rather opaque.[29] Two conferences, organised by the Hudson Institute in 1999 and 2000 in Washington, DC, and Berkshire, brought together what one journalistic observer called 'the intellectual heart of British-American conservatism'.[30] Among the delegates were Thatcher and David Davis MP (later the government minister tasked with negotiating the UK's departure from the EU), leading intellectual conservatives, including Francis Fukuyama, Robert Conquest and Kenneth Minogue, prominent commentators such as James C. Bennett, John O'Sullivan and Owen Harries, the media mogul Conrad Black, and John Hulsman from the Heritage Foundation. Very few American politicians identified with this cause in these years, with the notable exception of the leading Republican Pat Buchanan. The linkages which these events established – between politicians, pundits and intellectuals – represented the latest in a long line of Anglo-American political communities stretching back to the late nineteenth century and the invention of the idea of the English-speaking peoples.

Some of the key contributors to these conferences subsequently wrote books and articles seeking to revive the Anglosphere idea, a number of which appeared in outlets owned by Black and Rupert Murdoch. Black himself appears to have been closely involved in the various activities of this network. Like Murdoch, he was deeply hostile to the EU and developed a keen interest in promoting Eurosceptic voices in British politics. In an article published in the American magazine *The National Interest*, Black argued that Britain was 'afflicted by an existential loneliness; shackled to Continental European economies', which 'are paying huge quantities of Danegeld to the urban masses and uneconomic small farmers [with] political traditions [that] are corporatist, not liberal.'[31] The answer to this situation, he declared, was for the British to rediscover their heritage: 'Britain is at the centre, geographically, culturally and politically, of an Atlantic community, whereas it is in all respects on the periphery of an exclusively or predominantly European order.' In a lecture he delivered in 1998, he argued that membership of the EU required an unacceptable loss of sovereignty for the UK, whereas closer association with a loose Anglosphere alliance would not.[32]

The British journalist John Lloyd, who attended some of these keynote conferences, sensed that such ideas might well become more widely resonant. He characterised this particular milieu as 'self-confident, vengeful, well-funded and very sharp'.[33] Soon it began to attract a wider set of voices and contributors, including – rather notably – from countries outside the Old Commonwealth. In a speech to the Oxford Union in July 2005, which caused considerable controversy in his own country and sent a ripple throughout Anglosphere circles, the Indian prime minister, Manmohan Singh, observed the imperial sources of many of India's assets and strengths, from its railroads to its democratic system. 'If there is one phenomenon on which the sun cannot set', he observed, 'it is the world of the English-speaking peoples, in which the people of Indian origin are the single largest component.'[34] His argument was a precursor to a more concerted examination of the – seemingly unlikely – proposition that India might become an important partner within a putative Anglosphere association, a position also advanced by the Tory MP Daniel Hannan.[35] In January 2011 the foreign affairs magazine *New Criterion* published a special issue on the Anglosphere with authors from a variety of countries, including an Indian commentator, Madhav Das Alapat.[36]

The geographical expansion of the Anglosphere idea also drew sustenance from a separate intellectual current – an emerging interest in re-evaluating the nature and impact of the empire, a focus which was associated particularly with the controversial account of liberal imperialism supplied by Anglo-American commentator Niall Ferguson.[37] And it was advanced too in the addition by the historian Andrew Roberts to Churchill's iconic volumes on the history of the English-speaking peoples, which appeared in 2007.[38]

Nor was this debate confined to Britain. Within Anglosphere circles more broadly, the desire to re-evaluate colonial rule and to trace its positive legacies, such as the establishment of the rule of law, the development of democratic institutions and the spread of ideas of liberty, became a commonplace in these years. According to the Canadian pundit Mark Steyn, 'The key regional powers in almost every corner of the globe are ... British-derived – from Australia to South Africa to India – and, even among the lesser players, as a general rule you're better off for having been exposed to British rule than not.'[39]

Intellectuals of the Anglosphere: Robert Conquest and James C. Bennett

A rich tapestry of thinking – about international politics, the global economy and the common heritage and political culture of the English-speaking peoples – emanated from the New Right Anglosphere in these years. And some of its outputs and key themes began to catch the attention of pundits and politicians beyond its inner circle. It was also associated increasingly with a small number of iconic figures who emerged as the leading exponents of this perspective. Here we briefly rehearse the key contributions made by two especially influential Anglosphere advocates – Robert Conquest and James C. Bennett.

A respected academic expert on the history of the Soviet Union, Conquest produced two iconic overviews of the twentieth century which provided significant intellectual foundations, and a degree of respectability, for the political and cultural arguments advanced in this milieu. In *Reflections on a Ravaged Century* he concluded that 'the political arrangements of the West are defective' and insisted that 'the European Union is not proving to be the factor of strength expected by some.'[40] The answer to this state of affairs was 'a more fruitful unity' between the Anglosphere nations and an international arrangement that would permit the exercise of sovereignty and the maintenance of national tradition. For Britain, maintaining these historic relations, which were built on cultural ties, common history and similar political institutions, was bound to become a more appealing pathway than fighting to retain its own sovereignty within the fundamentally alien model of law and governance associated with the 'creeping federalisation' and overly bureaucratic character of the EU. But he urged sceptics to look harder at the already existing alternative arising from an ingrained set of historic ties to other English-speaking countries.

Conquest's sweeping vision was rooted in his rich historical perspective, as he returned his readers to the dilemmas and dreams of Churchill and the other architects of the international system after the Second World War. This was a vision rooted in history and common culture and did not carry a 'racial implication'. The UK, Conquest believed, ought to remain within the EU while joining this new association of Anglosphere states, reprising its mid-century role as bridge-builder and guide to both sides of this relationship.

Conquest provided an unusual account of how this alliance might work in his next major work, *Dragons of Expectation*, which included one of the very few concrete indications of how an Anglosphere association might be organised.[41] This would comprise a proportionally representative consultative council (the executive) and a larger assembly that would include foreign affairs, military, economic, social affairs, and legal and constitutional committees. The president of the association would be the president of the United States, 'as the largest and most powerful member', and 'the Queen, as head of state of so many component nations ..., should have a titular precedence, such as Queen of the Association.' This was, he readily admitted, a work of 'cultural and political science fiction',[42] not a fully worked-out proposal. The composition of the putative consultative council is itself revealing, with the USA allocated five seats, the UK two, and all other members just one.

Conquest's contention that such an arrangement was both desirable and, contrary to conventional wisdom, viable was closely connected to his belief that the EU was likely to fade in significance in world affairs. This prospect, and the inadequacy of the broader architecture of global governance in the face of the new challenges of the post-Cold War era, underpinned the need for such an association, which would ultimately provide a beacon for 'all parts of the world around which states sharing in any degree our aims of human liberty and progress, or needing support against our mutual enemies, may rally.'[43]

Conquest's thinking gained numerous intellectual and political admirers, including Thatcher, as she began to identify publicly with his ideas out of office. In her address to the English-Speaking Union in 1999 she unequivocally endorsed Conquest's thinking, remarking that 'such an international alliance ... would redefine the political landscape' and, in the long term, transform 'politically backward areas [by] creating the conditions for a genuine world community'.[44] Like him, she drew a sharp contrast between the dynamism and cultural community associated with the Anglosphere, on the one hand, and the EU, on the other, which lacked the deeper set of shared values that had for so long sustained the Anglo-American and Anglosphere ideals. With tongue slightly in cheek, she reminded her audience that 'God separated Britain from mainland Europe, and it was for a purpose.'[45] She also revisited the vision developed by Churchill of Anglo-America as bedrock for the Western order in the post-war world. But now, with the fall of the Berlin Wall and the demise of the Cold War – both victories that she unequivocally claimed for the English-speaking peoples – Thatcher offered considerable encouragement to those pursuing the Anglosphere as a geo-political and economic alternative to European integration.

Thatcher's public commitment to these ideas represented a notable shift in her own outlook and was prompted by her sharp turn against the EU. But there was continuity too in some of the sentiments she expressed, not least in terms of her own ongoing commitment to the Atlanticist ideal, which was still, in her mind, the core of the Anglosphere.

Now blessed by Thatcher, this cause became of increasing interest to a new generation of Eurosceptic Conservative politicians and commentators, including David (later Lord) Howell, John Redwood, Daniel Hannan, David Davis, Norman Lamont, Liam Fox, Bill Cash, David Willetts and Michael Howard.

While Conquest's work was an important conduit to the growing intellectual respectability and political traction of the Anglosphere idea in Britain, the work of another key contributor to many of these debates is suggestive of a different direction in which these arguments also moved – towards the potential associated with new communications technologies. James C. Bennett, a successful businessman and tech entrepreneur, wrote the most widely read books about this topic in this period. In *The Anglosphere Challenge* he argued that the nineteenth century was the high point of British pre-eminence and that the twentieth witnessed the rise of American power. The current century could well turn into a century also dominated by these Anglophone countries, now working in concert. For Bennett, economic and technological change made the Anglosphere a particularly viable proposition.[46] In an increasingly networked age, a common, English-derived culture is becoming more, not less, important as the foundation for economic cooperation, political allegiance and military coordination.[47]

Bennett has invested considerable energy in describing this shared cultural inheritance and the implications it carries for democratic governance, the rule of law and the idea of freedom. At its heart he discerns an enduring vein of individualism, and he connects this to the emergence of a form of government that respects liberty and promotes the forms of order in which the latter flourishes. In broad terms, he suggested, these norms have persisted in English-speaking countries during the era of mass immigration, but he remained concerned that the pursuit of multiculturalism in these countries could well undermine the kind of 'national cohesion' which has permitted the reproduction of such values over time. His culturally focused account was clearly distinguished from the notions of ethnic kinship which shaped earlier conceptions of the Anglosphere. It was memes not genes that undergirded the connections between these countries in the digital age. And the emergence of rising economies such as India and Ireland, where an English inheritance was still palpable, made them attractive allies in this enterprise.[48]

Bennett's most distinctive contribution to this genre of writing is the contention that digital and other technological advances are tearing down geographical barriers and opening up new opportunities for trade across vast distances. Having previously taken this argument in the direction espoused by other intellectual proponents of globalisation – towards assertions of the merits of global civil society and governance – he began to assert the importance of the institutional and cultural underpinnings that free markets require, which are most commonly associated with countries that were the beneficiaries of the English tradition. Greater economic cooperation among the Anglosphere nations would presage the emergence of a loose association of like-minded countries which would, in turn, supply a more authentic and robust defence of Western values than existing institutions or alliances were able to do. Writing in the early 2000s, Bennett offered a qualified judgement about whether the EU might succeed in establishing a free trade zone, noting its limited success in enabling the free movement of people, capital and ideas. But, echoing other Conservatives, he warned against its growing interventionism in areas of social policy and the tendency to distribute executive power away from national bodies under democratic scrutiny to unaccountable bodies at the EU level.

Bennett contrasted this bureaucratic and artificial project with the more organic forms of cooperation that characterised relations between countries within the Anglosphere. One of the signature arguments is his identification of an 'English-speaking network civilisation' associated with newspapers, blogs, commentators and ideas. He put much store too in the 'Five Eyes' intelligence-sharing scheme and a large number of regional institutions which link English-speaking states. This dense network of institutional and cultural relationships provides a platform from which further cooperative arrangements could readily be built. It was a theme picked up and echoed, enthusiastically, by others.[49] John O'Sullivan, a British columnist sympathetic to Bennett's vision, noted the 'definite pattern' to the forms of cooperation that linked these countries, which might well prepare the way for Bennett's network civilisation.[50] In due course, he suggested, governments may well come to see the value of such linkages and develop them in more conscious ways.

Conclusion

The most significant fault line running through the thinking of this transnational community of Anglosphere advocates concerned questions about strategy rather than goals. Did propounding the seemingly utopian goal of a formalised alliance among these far-flung states risk damaging its appeal to those who might otherwise identify with many of the values that Bennett and Conquest advocated? Contrary to those, such as Conquest, who have argued the merits of a formal federation, other champions of this cause have taken a very different tack. In his widely read book, for instance, Hannan went out of his way to distance himself from such ideas, suggesting that common approaches to policy, closer trade and a similar political economy would over time result in greater convergence.[51]

And yet, without evidence of any shift towards the institutional expression of the Anglosphere, the danger is that this notion looks both utopian and resolutely fictional – a preoccupation of parts of the transatlantic political and economic elites. Securing this as an important form of imagined community that can compete with the various other attachments and forms of connection that have become so important in the early twenty-first century among the populations of these disparate countries remains a major challenge for exponents of this idea.

Yet, the emergence of this body of writing and argument, and the championing of this ideal by influential figures in politics and the media, began to reach wider audiences and was gradually noted and engaged by more mainstream media figures. Above all, this current sustained the growing belief that there was a potential answer to the difficult question posed by supporters of the UK's membership of the EU: what might be the better alternative to it? Sketchy and underdeveloped as the notion of an alliance of the English-speaking peoples has often been, its advocates were able to demonstrate a real historical lineage for it and to make it look like the basis for a better tomorrow for Britain. Through the work of figures such as Bennett and Conquest, in particular, the fusion of Anglospheric thinking and neo-liberal ideas emerged as a vibrant ideological pattern. Both thinkers sought to take this idea away from its close association with the era and ethos of empire.

6

The Eurosceptic Anglosphere Emerges

In the two decades after the fall of the Berlin Wall, proponents of the Anglosphere were required to reorientate their ambitions in the wake of some profound shifts in the global economy and the political environments in which they were operating. In the 1990s, American capitalist democracy was indisputably dominant, ideologically and economically. Globalisation under the aegis of American liberalism was the 'given' of most economic arguments and political discourse. But new challenges to American power were also emerging. In Asia, China had begun its spectacular rise, while in the Middle East there were ominous signs that new conflicts were stirring. Then, at the turn of the new century, a bloody period of terror and war erupted that would reshape world politics, followed in short order by the end of the long economic boom and the global financial meltdown of 2007–8. These events would produce powerful new political cleavages in the USA on issues relating to national identity, defence and security; the Anglo-American model of capitalism; and the country's role in the wider world.

They also spilled over into the domestic politics of the UK. In the early 1990s, Thatcherism was a spent force and

Eurosceptics were politically divided and relatively marginal. The New Labour government elected in 1997 became the torchbearer for globalisation and positioned itself as the closest international ally to the USA and as a bridge between America and Europe. It oversaw the Labour Party's longest ever spell in office and presided over a lengthy period of economic growth. But, over time, it lost support – first, over the Iraq War; then over the substantial rise in migration to the UK that followed the accession to the European Union of Poland and other Eastern European states in 2004; and, finally, over the financial crisis itself, when it was punished as the incumbent administration at a moment of acute economic distress. When Labour lost power in 2010, a new phase in Eurosceptic politics opened up, and the Anglosphere was now central to it.

Looking through 'Five Eyes': The Politics of the Anglosphere

British Eurosceptics did have one important advantage during New Labour's lengthy tenure in office: conservative governments were soon in office in the USA, Canada, Australia and New Zealand. In the USA, George Bush Jr served two terms between 2001 and 2009. In 1996, John Howard was elected prime minister of Australia, ushering in a period of Liberal-led government that was to last until 2007. In 2006, Stephen Harper became prime minister of a minority Conservative government in Canada; he was re-elected twice and governed until 2015. And, in New Zealand, the National Party was in power under Jim Bolger between 1990 and 1997 and then again under John Key's premiership from 2008.

During the long years of Labour rule in the UK, these governments provided a sympathetic international milieu around which the peripatetic ranks of think-tankers, MPs, intellectuals, media moguls and business donors associated with the Anglosphere could develop their networks, ideas and influence. The model for this kind of transnational Anglophone communion had been cast by Lionel Curtis in the first half of the twentieth century. Curtis worked variously as a government adviser, an Oxford don, a political pamphleteer and an author and was the prime mover in the Round Table movement and founder of the Royal Institute of International Affairs (popularly known as Chatham House). In the course of all this activity, he travelled regularly in the British dominions. Although few have matched his prolific output and influence, later Anglosphere enthusiasts were often following in his footsteps, though travelling towards a very different destination. As we saw in chapter 1, Curtis ended his career supporting union in Europe and a wider international Western federation. The architects of the twenty-first-century Anglosphere were developing arguments in favour of dismantling the European bloc and promoting a new, Atlanticist world order.

John Howard was a leading figure in this new political constellation. A staunch monarchist, he was an enthusiast for Australia's British heritage, which he drew upon as a store of values and institutions that formed the political and cultural core of Australian identity. Leading an ethnically diverse country whose economy had become deeply integrated into the wider East Asian region, Howard could not afford either to reject multiculturalism overtly (he had done so to his cost as leader of the Liberal opposition in the 1980s and did not want to repeat the experience) or to assert an explicitly Anglospheric foreign policy orientation that would alienate his regional neighbours. He therefore refused 'to put Australia into any sphere – Anglo or otherwise' or to accept that Australia had to 'choose between its history and geography'.[1] But over his period in office he began consciously to assert the 'Anglo-Saxon' basis of Australia's shared values and to deepen its alliances with the countries of the Anglosphere.

This reorientation was most marked after the 9/11 attacks, which took place when Howard was on a diplomatic visit to the USA. He immediately invoked the ANZUS pact and committed Australian troops to support the Americans, first in Afghanistan and later in Iraq. In a speech given to the Heritage Foundation in 2010 after he had left office, Howard argued that 'those values that bind us to the United States and the other members of the Anglosphere ... are so very powerful and will always come through separately and apart from the other links that might exist between our country and other parts of the world.'[2] A firm advocate of the supremacy of nation-states in global politics, Howard prioritised bilateral trade deals with major economic partners such as the USA over multilateral trade negotiations and (notoriously) asserted national sovereignty in disputes over Australia's treatment of asylum seekers and refugees. On trade policy, immigration and fidelity to American leadership, Howard provided templates for British Conservatives and Eurosceptics. He announced his support for Brexit in early 2016.

Although elected just as Howard was leaving office, Stephen Harper shared many of the former's ideological predilections. Like Howard, he was sceptical of the UN and other multilateral institutions and reorientated Canadian foreign policy towards a number of broadly neo-conservative positions. He too was strongly monarchist and promoted the symbols of Canada's allegiance to the crown, restoring the royal titles to the Canadian Air Force and Navy and ordering Queen Elizabeth II's portrait to be hung in diplomatic missions abroad. The first prime minister from the Canadian New Right, Harper pursued a consciously counter-hegemonic strategy against the bastions of Canadian liberalism, challenging what he considered its bias towards Eastern Canadian economic interests, its dominance over the federal public administration, its accommodation of Quebecois nationalism, and its internationalist and environmentalist *Weltanschauung*. This earned him the full-throated admiration of some British Eurosceptics. Writing admiringly of Harper, Daniel

Hannan called him 'perhaps the most pro-British and pro-American leader in the world', who had brought Canadians 'back to their old ways' of rugged, small-state and martial virtues and jettisoned the 'goody-two shoes officious Canada', with its support for multiculturalism and the United Nations. Under Harper, he wrote, Canada had 'convincingly rejoined the Anglosphere'.[3]

From the very outset of his time in office, Harper employed Churchillian points of reference, declaring 'the "little island" and the "Great Dominion" ... eternally bonded by language, culture, economics and values'. Speaking to the Canadian–UK Chamber of Commerce in 2006, Harper adduced all the core themes of what James Bennett called the 'unique societal template' of the Anglosphere: shared language, the common law, the free market economy, basic freedoms and parliamentary democracy, all linked together by Churchill's 'golden circle of the crown' and culturally enrobed by 'Shakespeare, Dickens, Kipling, Lewis, and Chesterton'.[4]

Political and ideological links between the Anglophone countries were not confined to conservatives, however. The British left's intellectual and political networks were also strongly orientated towards the Anglosphere in this period, especially the USA and Australia. In the early 1990s, Bill Clinton's victory in the 1992 US presidential election and his ideological reinvention as a 'New Democrat' exercised a magnetic attraction for Labour's self-styled modernisers. Labour's electoral strategists followed the 1992 presidential campaign closely, observing how Clinton positioned himself as a centrist 'Third Way' candidate who was critical of both free market conservatism and New Deal liberalism and was ruthless in closing down traditional sources of political weakness for the Democrats on the economy, crime and national security. Mesmerised by Clinton's political and economic successes, Labour cemented its US links in the later 1990s, building strong personal relationships with Democrat politicians and pollsters, facilitating collaborations between think-tanks, and recruiting advisers who had done stints at Harvard University's Kennedy School. A dense network of elite alliances – intellectual, political and financial – was forged with key American figures that would be carried into office when Labour won the 1997 general election. These were to become important as the UK turned to the USA for help in relation to the Northern Irish peace process and worked closely with it in Kosovo and the Middle East.[5]

At the same time, Labour looked south, to Australia, where the Hawke and Keating governments of 1983 to 1996 were seen by some as Third Way administrations *avant le lettre*.[6] The Commission on Social Justice, run by the UK think-tank the Institute for Public Policy Research at the instigation of the British Labour Party's leadership, drew heavily on Australian employment, welfare to work and student finance policies in its 1994 report, *Social Justice: Strategies for National Renewal*.[7] The Australian Labour Party's long run in government, and its success in winning a fifth term in office at the 1993 federal election after a severe recession, was a particular source of inspiration for Labour. In later years, when their political fortunes were reversed, rising figures in the Australian Labour Party, such as its future prime minister Kevin Rudd, were regular visitors to centre-left political meetings and think-tank seminars in London.

These political networks were facilitated by commonalities of thinking about political economy, welfare states and structures of governance, connections which deepened as a consequence of the neo-liberal turn in the political cultures of a number of these countries, notably the UK, the USA, New Zealand and Australia. The doctrines of the 'New Public Management' paradigm, and its techniques of quasi-market reform for public services, became widely diffused in the Anglosphere countries, providing a common set of ideas about the restructuring of public administration. Policy transfer was facilitated too by various shared institutional features of the Anglophone countries, including low rates of unionisation and

deregulated labour markets; market competition rather
than sector coordination between firms; short-termist
capital investment, typically accessed via stockmarkets,
rather than patient finance; shareholder dominance of
corporate governance; a reliance on academic or general
education rather than strong vocational training; and high
rates of means-testing and the private provision of welfare.
These features form part of the landscape of Andrew Gamble's 'Anglo-America' – a dense ensemble of market, state,
cultural and ideological institutions and practices. This
sustained a 'distinctive architecture of policy collaboration
between these countries', consisting of transgovernmental
elite policy networks addressing common problems and
devising shared solutions. Its depth and range suggests a
'structural multilateral relationship in the Anglosphere,
rather than simply bilateral or ad hoc arrangements.'[8]

From the 'End of History' to Iraq

In the immediate years after the collapse of Soviet communism, when Francis Fukuyama's contention that liberal-
democratic capitalism represented the 'end of history', the
global dominance of this Anglo-American, liberal economic and political order appeared assured. A long boom,
fuelled by global financialisation, was under way. China
and India were becoming integrated into the global
economy. And some of the leading, disruptive ideologies
of the twentieth century – fascism, communism and social-
ism – had apparently fallen away. The 'Washington Consensus' dominated decision-making in the world's economic
institutions. American military supremacy was unrivalled.
The liberal, free market institutional order appeared to
contain no internal contradictions that could threaten it.
The prospect of a serious challenge to the Anglo-American
West was almost inconceivable.

Fukuyama captured the Zeitgeist of this moment with
great elan, anchoring the claims of liberal democratic

politics and Anglo-liberal capitalism in a historicist account which foretold their continued dominance into the new century. Yet, precisely because of its universalist aspirations, Fukuyama's thinking eschewed any recourse to Anglosphere Whiggishness. The spread of democracy and the market could not be reduced, culturally or institutionally, to the genius of the English-speaking peoples. Instead, the motor of history was to be found in a potent combination of science and the soul, the advance of technology and the desire for equality of social recognition. In combination, the power of science and the desire for equal worth were the master keys of liberal democracy's triumph. This held true for democracies around the world, not just Anglo-American ones.

The sting in Fukuyama's tail was that the 'last man' produced by the liberal democratic terminus of history could be less than fully human, perhaps even an object of contempt: 'Is there not a side of the human personality that deliberately seeks out struggle, danger, risk, and daring, and will this side not remain unfulfilled by the "peace and prosperity" of contemporary liberal democracy?', he asked.[9] This question was answered in a little over a decade, when the illusion of prosperity and security was shattered by the 9/11 attacks and the wars in Afghanistan and Iraq that followed. The end of history would be replaced by a war seemingly without end – the 'War on Terror'.

This new conflagration crystallised a set of ideological debates about American foreign policy that would bear directly – and disastrously for the British Labour Party – on the politics of the Anglosphere. Although he would come to disown this affiliation, Fukuyama was originally a leading light in the neo-conservative movement in the United States after 9/11. Neo-conservatives responded to the New York attacks by launching a campaign for armed intervention and regime change in Iraq, presaged in part on a belief that democracy could be imposed by military force, and that US military supremacy was so overwhelming that it could not be resisted. The neo-conservatives reflected the universalistic hubris of Fukuyama's vision and directed it towards a new military strategy.

In doing so, they rejected the advice of foreign policy 'realists', who were sceptical of intervention in Iraq, and of cultural conservatives, who argued that American democracy was the product of a particular history centred on the culture and institutions of Anglo-Protestantism, not a universal form of government that could be exported around the world. It was part of a 'West' that was very unlike 'the Rest'. The USA was a major part of a civilisation, with a strong dispositional core which, as Samuel Huntington put it, was engaged in a 'clash of civilisations'. And this conflict required the West to cultivate its own coherence, dynamism and security, not intervene in the affairs of others. 'In a multipolar, multicivilizational world, the West's responsibility is to secure its own interests', wrote Huntington, 'not to promote those of other peoples nor to attempt to settle conflicts between other peoples when those conflicts are of little or no consequence to the West.'[10] On this account, neo-conservatism was liberal imperialism in a new guise, seeking to remake the world in America's image, just as liberal cosmopolitanism was trying to remake America in the world's image. Both visions, he argued, were fundamentally misguided. The USA should protect and nurture its indigenous national heritage: ethnically inclusive, yet defined by its Anglo-Protestant cultural core and its religious inheritance, and realist, not confrontational, on the world stage.

In the immediate aftermath of the 9/11 attacks, these ideological divisions were not yet apparent. The USA and its NATO allies invoked Article 5 of the North Atlantic Treaty, which commits its signatories to assist parties to the treaty that have been attacked, including, if they so decided, by the use of force. The subsequent deployment of force in Afghanistan against al-Qaeda bases and the Taliban government gathered both broad international support and material military commitment from NATO countries. Intellectually, ideologically and politically, the military response to the al-Qaeda threat enjoyed wide-ranging support. Huntington's 'clash of civilisations' was widely thought to have foretold the nature of this emerging conflict. The War on Terror would be fought, not against Islam or Muslim populations across the world, but against a particular group of defined aggressors and those shelter-ing them.

The decision to invade Iraq provoked a split in this coalition of support, forcing into the open debates about the role of the United States in the world, the nature of its War on Terror and the allies upon which it could call. And it divided the Anglosphere down the middle. Canada's liberal government broke ranks with Washing-ton, as it had done over Cuba and Vietnam, and refused to commit resources to the invasion. But it did not adopt a high-profile or principled opposition to the war, and its policy processes in response to it were rather muddled. It sought neither to alienate its powerful neighbour nor publicly to support it.[11] New Zealand, under the lead-ership of the Labour prime minister Helen Clark, also stayed out of the invasion on the grounds that military force did not have UN authorisation, while Ireland's historic commitment to neutrality prevented it from participating directly in the war. In contrast, Australia joined the action, though its military commitment was in practice limited.

In the Anglophone world, the Iraq War generated the deepest political divisions – and most bitter legacy – in the UK. Tony Blair's government saw its role as one of steer-ing the United States towards securing multilateral support and UN authorisation for the invasion, while invoking the special relationship to construct a bridge between Europe and the USA and seeking to reinvigorate the Middle East peace process. In each of these objectives it failed. The French government refused to back a second Iraq resolu-tion in the UN Security Council, and Europe was split in two by the war. Instead of uniting the 'Euroamerican'

West, as Huntington had termed it, the Americans' determination to topple Saddam Hussein drew a geo-political line between what some called 'Old' and 'New' Europe – those who opposed the invasion and those who supported it. In the UK itself, the decision to join the war split the Labour government, its supporters and the country at large.

Initially, at least, Eurosceptic enthusiasts for the Iraq War drew sustenance from the divisions it engendered, reading the alliance between the UK and the USA, and the refusal of key European governments to join the so-called Coalition of the Willing, as confirmation of both the underlying unity of Anglo-America and Great Britain's irreducible differences with continental Europe. The reluctance of Canada and New Zealand to take their place in the Anglosphere fold could be attributed to the liberal inclinations of the governments in both places. John Howard, meanwhile, had ably demonstrated that 'muscular conservative' leaders had no qualms about supporting the Anglo-American cause.

The descent into deadly violence in Iraq brought the tensions between different visions of the US-led world order back to the fore. Realists reasserted their foreign policy paradigm in Washington, pointing to the carnage in Iraq to denounce the perils of neo-conservative adventurism. Fukuyama famously parted company with his erstwhile allies, and other leading supporters of the war, such as the historian Niall Ferguson, recanted their earlier enthusiasm and lined up behind the new realist disposition. Liberal interventionism – including the Gladstonian tradition that Tony Blair had revived to justify the interventions in Kosovo and Sierra Leone – also sank into the Iraqi quagmire. Public scepticism towards overseas wars grew considerably, and in 2008 Barack Obama was elected president on a pledge to pull the USA out of Iraq. Talk of the War on Terror – if not the military and intelligence operations against al-Qaeda and its affiliates and heirs – was abandoned in the UK and the USA.

Rescuing the Anglosphere

But, far from collapsing under the weight of this dramatic history, the political idea of the Anglosphere was rescued and then revived in the post-Iraq War years, re-emerging as a leading paradigm for parts of the political and foreign policy communities. The first, and perhaps most ingenious, attempt to give Anglo-America a new ideological foundation after Iraq came from the public intellectual and foreign policy strategist Walter Russell Mead, in his book *God and Gold: Britain, America and the Making of the Modern World* (2007).[12] Mead set American economic and political power in an unbroken Anglo-American lineage, one that could be traced back to the Glorious Revolution in 1688 which had established the basis for parliamentary and Protestant rule in Britain. Ever since then, he argued, the 'Anglo-Americans have been on the winning side in every major international conflict.' A unique constellation of civilisational characteristics, combining a dynamic Protestant inheritance with the institutions and practices of a free market economy and democratic government, gave Anglo-America the relentless capacity to innovate, advance and dominate. At the heart of this inheritance sat the Whig narrative of progress, linking capitalist development and military success to the unfolding will of God. At each moment of world-historical crisis, the Anglosphere world prevailed, whether over Napoleon, the Kaiser, Hitler or the Soviet Union. And after each victory, Mead argued, the Anglo-Saxons believed they had reached the end of history. Optimism is the default setting of this worldview. 'How could it not be? The Whig narrative teaches us plainly that God is on our side, and centuries of victorious experience and economic progress confirm that the message is right.'[13]

Underpinning this hegemony is what Mead called the 'maritime order'. Plundering the tradition of naval military strategy pioneered by Alfred Mahan, Mead rooted Anglo-American global dominance in control of the sea, whose lanes link the strategic theatres of the world. 'Whoever controls the sea can choose the architecture that shapes the world', he argued.[14] A maritime system is more than simply naval power, however; it is an interconnected economic and geo-political system that simultaneously opens up the world to trade, secures its key networks, and enables the flexible deployment of military resources to where they are needed. It would, in short, enable global hegemony.

The end of history itself is an illusion, however. After each climactic victory, the cycle of crisis and war returns. Anglo-American liberal capitalist democracy generates accelerated change, not just within its heartlands but throughout the rest of the world into which it restlessly reaches. This breeds insecurity, resentment and resistance, Mead argued, not least in many Muslim societies, which increasingly consider American power and the maritime system to be illegitimate. Instead of invoking pieties about human rights, liberal economics and the moral law, Mead wrote, Anglo-America needed to practise a new 'diplomacy of civilisations' and engage much more deeply and thoughtfully with the Arab world.

Mead supplied an important and influential recasting of the Anglosphere that insisted upon the cultural, institutional and religious distinctiveness of a continuous Anglo-American lineage, but which simultaneously sought to explain (and constrain) its persistent overreach. It embraced Huntington's insistence of civilisational difference but layered over it the inevitability of Anglo-liberal capitalist penetration into the wider world, coating realism with a missionary moralistic sensibility. After the cataclysm of Iraq, it set out to equip America with a purposive, yet also realist, international statecraft: Nixonian *Realpolitik* blended with Wilsonian idealism.[15]

This recasting clearly suited the return to realism in Obama's foreign policy. But it also helped rescue the vision of Anglo-America as a progressive and powerful force in world history from the debris of Iraq. This was an important ideological pivot for British Conservative

Eurosceptics, whose primary interest now shifted from foreign policy to the construction of a new horizon of possibility for the UK outside the European Union. After the 2010 general election, when Labour's long stretch in government was finally brought to an end, discussion of the Anglosphere as a serious alternative to the EU began to intensify in the Conservative Party and the penumbra of think-tanks, political magazines, lobbying groups and public intellectuals surrounding it.

This intensification of interest was stimulated in part by the rise in support for the United Kingdom Independence Party (UKIP), which had seen significant electoral gains in European parliamentary elections in 2004 and 2009, and which was starting to win increased support (if not seats) at Westminster elections. Under the leadership of Nigel Farage it had established itself as a radical right-wing populist party, surfing public anxiety about immigration and feeding off traditionalist conservative disillusionment with social liberalism. In the 2014 European Parliament elections, it topped the poll, with over a quarter of the votes cast. Its rise was the single most important factor behind David Cameron's decision to commit his party to a referendum on the UK's membership of the EU.

UKIP manifestos in this period repeatedly emphasised Britain's Commonwealth history and ties, which, it argued, had been 'shamefully betrayed and neglected by previous governments'. At the 2010 general election, UKIP positioned itself as 'the Party of the Commonwealth', arguing for a Commonwealth Free Trade Area. In 2015, it made explicit reference to the Anglosphere:

> Britain is not merely a European country, but part of a global community, the Anglosphere. Beyond the EU and even the Commonwealth are a network of nations that share not merely our language but our common law, democratic traditions and global trading interests. From India to the United States, New Zealand to the Caribbean, UKIP would want to foster closer ties with the Anglosphere.[16]

The reference to India is a telling one. The dramatic growth of Asian economies in the 1990s and 2000s allowed Eurosceptics to argue that trade outside the EU was becoming more important to the UK than trade within the European bloc – much as Chamberlainites at the start of the twentieth century had argued that the white settler dominions were the fastest growing economies of the future. Britain's imperial heritage could now be reinvented as an asset for the future. Former colonial territories such as India, Singapore and Hong Kong could be embraced as a part of the Anglosphere constellation, enabling Britain to exploit her past to strike new trade deals with the global markets of the future. For neo-Thatcherites, the added advantage was that Asian economies had less developed welfare states and lower levels of labour and product markets regulation than countries within the EU. They were models of fiscal rectitude and welfare state retrenchment and were associated with the lauded 'Asian' virtues of thrift, hard work and self-reliance. An Asian pivot within Anglosphere discourse therefore enabled arguments about the UK's political economy and trading policies to be brought together: free trade outside the EU customs union and a smaller central state would ensure the potential for Britannia to be 'Unchained', as the title of a pamphlet written in 2012 by a group of Conservative MPs put it.

With Conservatives now in power in the UK once more, the advocacy of the Anglosphere moved into the British political mainstream. The foreign secretary, William Hague, sought to deepen military and intelligence cooperation with the 'Five Eyes' states and put particular energy into renewing Britain's diplomatic ties with Australia, which he visited on several occasions during his tenure in office. On giving the 2013 John Howard Lecture in New South Wales, Hague affirmed 'the ties of history, family, and values' binding Australia and Great Britain together and sought to position both countries as regional actors with global links.[17] On a trip to Australia in 2013, Boris Johnson, then mayor of London, struck a distinctly

Eurosceptic tone, rehearsing the argument that Britain had betrayed its relationships with the Commonwealth in 1973 and arguing that the UK should seek greater links with the dynamic growing economies of the new world. He proposed a 'Free Labour Mobility Zone' with Australia.[18] In 2014, he would return to this theme, arguing that 'it is absurd that we should be kicking out Australian physiotherapists and nurses and teachers, and excluding New Zealand scientists, our kith and kin as we used to say.'[19]

This was political positioning intended largely for a domestic audience – a foretaste of what was to come when Johnson would break ranks with his prime minister and join the Leave campaign in the 2016 EU referendum. The new leader of the Australian Liberal Party, British-born Tony Abbott, who served as prime minister of Australia between 2013 and 2015, warmly reciprocated Hague and Johnson's sentiments. Abbott was an enthusiast for the Anglosphere and argued in a speech in Oxford in 2012 that, 'As with all the countries that think and argue among themselves in English (that these days include Singapore and Hong Kong, Malaysia and even India), what we have in common is usually more important than anything that divides us.'[20] For Antipodean conservatives, embracing the Asian countries that were once part of the British Empire made perfect sense.

Towards the EU Referendum

With Stephen Harper, Tony Abbott and John Key all in office at the same time as a Conservative-led coalition in the UK, and the prospect of an impending Brexit referendum, the gravitational pull of the Anglosphere on the political imagination of neo-liberal Eurosceptics intensified. Politicians, commentators and think-tanks such as the Institute of Economic Affairs and the Adam Smith Institute, which had long-established transatlantic ties with Washington counterparts such as the Heritage Foundation, the Cato Institute and the American Enterprise Institute, began to publish pamphlets, speeches and blogs making the case for Brexit. These typically reimagined Britain as a freewheeling, globally networked economy, striking trade deals with the USA, Canada and an expanded Asian and Australasian Anglosphere. Arguments that would subsequently be played out during the Brexit referendum were first rehearsed in these quarters.

At the core of these arguments was a very distinctive economic vision. The financial crisis of 2008–9 had blown a large hole in the intellectual edifice of Anglo-American capitalism. But, in its immediate aftermath, a combination of quantitative easing, the judicious application of Keynesian fiscal prescriptions and massive Chinese credit creation helped pull the US, UK and Asian economies out of recession. In contrast, structural imbalances and the bursting of property bubbles in the eurozone triggered sovereign debt crises that exposed the deep flaws in the architecture of the single currency. These elicited in response the implementation of forms of austerity which drove the deficit countries of Europe into a prolonged period of chronic stagnation and mass unemployment. Since countries belonging to the single currency no longer had available to them economic policy instruments such as devaluation or fiscal stimulus, their ability to respond to the crisis was brutally curtailed. The EU's economic and democratic legitimacy were both significantly impaired.

These developments were a boon for Eurosceptics. In contrast to the referendum in 1975, Europe's 'output legitimacy' was seriously weakened. Where relative economic decline had once driven British political elites to seek entry to a prosperous European market, now the economic position was apparently reversed. The eurozone was in terminal decline, and the Anglosphere, embracing the Asian Commonwealth, was on the rise, it was increasingly said.[21] With the USA at its heart, the Anglosphere would constitute the world's largest economic bloc, at over a quarter of global GDP. It was being replenished by immigration, whereas Europe was ageing and was now, truly, the old continent. The Anglosphere was militarily dominant and its linguistic supremacy endowed it with powerful forms of cultural, intellectual and geo-political 'soft power'.[22] Liberated from the EU, the UK could take up its place at the heart of this new potential bloc.

There were strong echoes of late Victorian debates in these arguments. Few advocates of the Anglosphere argued for formal political union – just as, in the late nineteenth century, the idea of an institutional federation appeared utopian and remote. But technology played a key role, in imaginative terms, just as it had for earlier proponents of Greater Britain, by collapsing the constraints associated with distance. Now it was the internet, not underwater cables, that would overcome the limitations of geography. The English-speaking alliance of the twenty-first century would be networked and cultural, not statist or ethno-centrist.

The USA remained problematic in these visions, just as it had done for Victorian British imperialists. Under Obama, the country had embarked on fiscal stimulus, banking reform and state-mandated extensions of health-care insurance, all of which were anathema to Tea Party activists and libertarian-leaning Republicans, as well as to their ideological counterparts in the UK. Pamphlets appeared denouncing Obama for taking the United States down the path of European statism.[23] And his administration returned to the default setting among US foreign policy-makers, supporting a united Europe with the UK a key member of it. This position also provoked some hostility among British Eurosceptics, who began to echo the kind of scepticism about the USA associated with Powell and other Conservatives.

At the same time, the prevailing weakness in Labour circles of a story about national purpose and identity in the UK, and a disinclination to take a clear stand on the European question, helped ensure that these ideas tended to pass unchallenged. During the 1980s, the Labour Party overcame its divisions on Europe and rejected the Euroscepticism of its socialist left in favour of a broadly pro-European, social democratic identity. Commitment to the EU became a marker of Labour's modernisation and was seen as a precondition for its rehabilitation as a party of the mainstream centre-left. Labour supported Britain's entry to the European ERM and the Maastricht Treaty, despite protests from some figures on the Keynesian 'soft left' (whose criticisms of the architecture of European monetary union turned out to be highly prescient). The wider Labour movement was won around to a pro-European position in the late 1980s by Jacques Delors, then president of the European Commission, whose support for the extension of workers' rights gave Britain's trade unions a reason to commend the European Union, not condemn it. By 1997, Euroscepticism in Labour circles had become a distinctly minority pastime.

Yet real enthusiasm for Europe was relatively rare on the Labour benches. Many of those who accompanied Roy Jenkins into the lobbies with the Heath government to support Britain's membership of the Common Market in the early 1970s also followed him into the Social Democratic Party in the 1980s. As it entered office after its wilderness years, Labour was left with few intellectual and political resources with which to negotiate the European question. Tony Blair's enthusiasm for Europe was tempered by his appreciation of the lack of popular enthusiasm for the EU and by the stark 'Euro-realism' of his chancellor and successor, Gordon Brown. The Third Way itself offered little thinking about national identity and purpose. These marked gaps in Labour's national outlook and political instincts were powerfully exposed in the years running up to the EU referendum.

7

Brexit: The Anglosphere Triumphant?

It was in early 2013, in a speech he delivered at Bloomberg in London, that David Cameron, the Conservative prime minister, announced that Britain would hold a referendum on its membership of the European Union, setting in train the events that would lead to the Brexit vote a few years later. Under pressure from the growing ranks of Eurosceptics within his own party, and the rise in support for UKIP outside it, Cameron argued that he wanted to negotiate a new settlement for Britain in Europe and then put it to the British people in a referendum. He got the electoral mandate to pursue this course when he secured a majority for his party at the 2015 general election and promptly opened negotiations with the rest of the EU.

The negotiations achieved little of substance, however. European leaders were not ready for treaty change and were preoccupied with the ongoing problems of the eurozone and the refugee crisis precipitated by the Syrian civil war. Cameron could secure only minor amendments to the social security entitlements of EU nationals migrating to the UK and several other, largely cosmetic reforms. This package of changes had very little impact upon the referendum debate that opened up early in 2016.

With the long-anticipated referendum on the UK's membership of the EU now imminent, proponents of the Anglosphere moved into a more overtly political mode of operation, drawing on their ideological reworking of Britain's global history to advance a new account of the country's role in the world outside the EU and establishing the key positions that would form the core of their referendum platform. The overarching rationale for these was supplied by Michael Gove, a long-time ally of the prime minister who decamped to help lead the official Vote Leave campaign alongside the former mayor of London, Boris Johnson. (Johnson would later unwittingly bestow a metaphor on the effect the Brexit referendum would have on his own party's leadership when he described the media scrum outside his house, as he announced his support for leaving the EU, as an 'imperial goatfuck'.)[1]

Gove built his case on the same foundations as those established by Powell in 1975, namely that Britain had lost her sovereignty by joining this wider union: 'our membership of the European Union prevents us being able to change huge swathes of law and stops us being able to choose who makes critical decisions which affect all our lives. Laws which govern citizens in this country are decided by politicians from other nations who we never elected and can't throw out.'[2] His appeal to sovereignty – often eliding the distinction between its popular and parliamentary forms – would be crystallised in the Vote Leave campaign slogan, 'Take Back Control'.

In terms that echoed late Victorian historians such as Edward A. Freeman, Gove traced Britain's liberal and parliamentary credentials back in a golden thread that ran throughout the centuries: 'In Britain we established trial by jury in the modern world, we set up the first free parliament, we ensured no-one could be arbitrarily detained at the behest of the Government, we forced our rulers to recognise they ruled by consent not by right ...' Yet, mindful of the broad political coalition that success in the Brexit referendum would demand, he added that 'we led

the world in abolishing slavery, we established free education for all, national insurance, the National Health Service
and a national broadcaster respected across the world.'[3]
Just like Chamberlain, the Vote Leave campaign knew that
it would be critical to enlist working-class support to their
cause. Broadening out the familiar 'island story' to embrace
the historical achievements of radicals and socialists was
one part of this strategy. And so too was a promise to
divert the UK's gross contributions to the EU of £350
million a week into the National Health Service. This
pledge was to become infamous, as it inflated the true cost
of Britain's membership of the European Union and was
ditched after the referendum, but it had significant resonance with parts of the electorate.

Gove gestured self-consciously towards the Anglosphere, arguing that 'as a result of [the efforts of radicals
and liberals] we developed, and exported to nations like
the US, India, Canada and Australia, a system of democratic self-government which has brought prosperity and
peace to millions.'[4] David Davis, a longstanding Eurosceptic, argued more forcibly in early 2016 that 'This is an
opportunity to renew our strong relationships with Commonwealth and Anglosphere countries. These parts of the
world are growing faster than Europe. We share history,
culture and language. We have family ties. We even share
similar legal systems. The usual barriers to trade are largely
absent.'[5] He and other Eurosceptics held up the Canada–
EU Comprehensive Economic and Trade Agreement
(CETA) as a model for a post-Brexit relationship between
Britain and the EU, together with the 'Australian Points
System' as an example of a sovereign immigration policy.

Yet, despite these fairly common Anglosphere references, Vote Leave strategists avoided deploying empire
nostalgia or Commonwealth sentimentality in the campaign itself: 'Take Back Control', more money for the
NHS, and an end to free movement in the EU were its key
proposals, relentlessly promoted. Conversely, slogans such
as 'Go Global' were ditched. In contrast to the public

debates that took place in the 1960s and 1970s on Britain's membership of the EEC, appeals to Commonwealth ties and obligations were rare in the 2016 referendum (aside from tactical promises to ethnic minority communities that Commonwealth countries could have priority in a post-Brexit immigration system). When Gove, Johnson and others did refer to the Commonwealth directly, they tended to invoke a global tradition that Britain had abandoned in the 1970s when it made the fateful decision to enter the Common Market, a preference that flowed from the declinist sentiments which, they argued, prevailed in that decade.

The Vote Leave campaign also sought to tap directly into popular anxieties about immigration by focusing on how membership of the EU prevented the UK from managing European migration flows, thereby yoking together the theme of popular sovereignty with that of border control. Dominic Cummings, adviser to Michael Gove and the main Vote Leave strategist, was clear about the centrality of immigration to the Brexit campaign:

> 15 years of immigration and, recently, a few years of the migration crisis from the East and Africa, dramatically portrayed on TV and social media, had a big effect. In 2000, focus groups were already unhappy with immigration but did not regard it as a problem caused by the EU. By 2015, the EU was blamed substantially for the immigration/asylum crisis and this was entangled with years of news stories about 'European courts' limiting action against terrorists and criminals.[6]

This was contentious territory. Within the disparate Brexiteer camp, the role of Nigel Farage, the UKIP leader, whose proclivity for stirring nativist, anti-immigration sentiments was well established, would prove a major source of friction. Yet, although the official Vote Leave campaign sidelined Farage and his supporters for fear of his unpopularity with parts of the electorate, it did not hold back from claiming that 'Turkey (Population 76 million) is joining the

EU' and that Britain's borders would soon 'extend to Iraq and Syria'. The xenophobic tenor of this message was not lost on anyone.

The legacy of British colonialism itself became a flash-point during the campaign when President Obama visited the UK and urged Britons to remain in the EU, pointedly noting in a press conference with Cameron that the country would go to the 'back of the queue' in free trade negotiations if it voted for Brexit. This brought protests from some Brexit campaigners that were redolent of the resentments directed at the USA by British imperialists throughout the twentieth century. This time, however, political hostility shaded into racism. Boris Johnson brought up claims that President Obama had removed a bust of Winston Churchill from the Oval Office because 'it was a symbol of the part-Kenyan president's ancestral dislike of the British Empire – of which Churchill had been such a fervent defender.' Nigel Farage waded in too, telling Obama to 'butt out' and arguing that the president's family came from a school of thought that saw the British as 'foreign invaders'.[7]

Obama was rehearsing the longstanding American view that the UK should remain inside an integrated European bloc, and he was prepared to intervene in the Brexit referendum to make his point. Leaders of other Anglosphere countries, from Canada's new prime minister, Justin Trudeau, to John Key in New Zealand and Australia's Malcolm Turnbull, voiced similar positions. Britain should stay inside the EU, they all argued. A former foreign secretary of Australia, Gareth Evans, mocked the 'bizarre argument' that 'a self-exiled UK will find a new global relevance, and indeed leadership role, as the centre of the Anglosphere.'[8] The English-speaking peoples outside Britain had apparently moved on from this older political lineage.

It was not just Britain's future but also her past that would become a source of political contestation during the referendum. In a sub-plot to the campaign, British historians became embroiled in arguments about the nature and provenance of the UK's relationship to Europe. They debated whether its historical experience was a unique one of largely uninterrupted, peaceful and democratic development, orientated towards the world more than the European continent, or instead whether it had always been enmeshed with Europe and had experienced violence, revolutionary upheaval and a relatively recent passage to democracy, just as its neighbours had done. A group of historians formed Historians for Britain – one of a number of such bodies set up under the umbrella of the Brexit campaign – and published a piece by David Abulafia, in *History Today*, arguing that 'Britain's unique history sets it apart from the rest of Europe.' This engendered a response from a rival group of historians, asserting that 'a history that emphasises Britain's differences and separation from Europe (or elsewhere) narrows and diminishes our parameters, making our history not exceptional but undernourished.'[9] Encapsulated in these scholarly arguments were the ideas and debates that had swirled around Britain's role in the world since the late Victorian era: whether it was a world island, with a tradition of durable, distinctive institutions that marked out its exceptionalism, or whether it was a power that had deep historical and cultural ties to Europe and centuries of involvement in its affairs which had always depended on European alliances to secure its global position.

When the referendum results were announced, longstanding fissures, as well as more recent post-industrial social divisions, were laid bare. Scotland voted 62 per cent to 38 per cent to remain in the EU, as did the people of Northern Ireland, by 55.8 per cent to 44.2 per cent, although sectarian divisions were evident in the breakdown of the vote, with nationalist communities voting to remain and many (if far from all) Unionist communities following the lead of the Democratic Unionist Party and voting to leave. England and Wales also voted to leave the EU, although London and a number of other large cities and university towns voted to remain. England-without-London voted to leave the EU by 55.4 per cent to 44.6 per cent. The result revealed a country divided by the cleavages of education, class, history and geography, but the divisions across the territories of the UK were especially stark. 'It was England's Brexit', declared the commentator and campaigner Anthony Barnett.[10]

The idea of the Anglosphere had remained largely in the background of the campaign, playing a subordinate role to the Vote Leave focus on democratic agency, immigration control and increased spending on the NHS. But it supplied a horizon of possibility and affective ideological content for many Brexiteers – a way of thinking about Britain's history and its place in the world outside the EU that gave emotive force to otherwise abstract economic, political and judicial arguments. The main drivers of the referendum result were a cocktail of long-term post-industrial decline, the fallout from the financial crisis, stagnant real wages, high and destabilising levels of immigration, and the crisis in the eurozone itself. Against this backdrop, the Stronger In campaign had been unable to convince a majority of voters that leaving was a risk too far and that Britain's future lay in Europe. It deployed largely instrumental and technocratic arguments and was unable to muster either a resonant appeal to current forms of nationhood or an appealing account of Britain's place and future in the world.

After the Referendum

The referendum result sent a shock wave around the countries of the EU. And in Britain it triggered a political crisis. Cameron resigned, setting in train an unpredictable and unexpected leadership contest. Its winner – Theresa May, an unenthusiastic supporter of 'Remain' – made the rapid delivery of Brexit her central political focus, a stance that put her political opponents on the back foot, especially the

Labour Party, which was deeply divided on this issue. The statement she delivered on the steps of Downing Street on her first day in office also signalled the advent of a new, but brief, period in British politics. Then, and subsequently, she promoted objectives associated with the Chamberlainite variant of one-nation Conservatism, including social reforms designed to address the declining economic position of working-class voters, greater state intervention in economic life and, above all, the reduction of levels of immigration into the UK.[11] In key respects, these positions clashed with the 'Global Britain' vision associated with the Thatcherite Eurosceptics who had promoted the Anglosphere to underpin the case for leaving the EU.

And yet, in other respects, the deep imprint of the Anglosphere lineage remains very apparent after Brexit. The dash by ministers in the months after the referendum to open discussions with various English-speaking governments about potential future trade deals – including Australia, India, New Zealand and the USA – suggested that the belief in the fundamental cultural and economic similarities between the UK and these countries has percolated deeply into Britain's state and politics. More generally, the Brexit vote has engendered a notable reconfiguration of the nature and terms of the debate about the UK's place in the world and where its future lies. And in this regard, too, the Anglosphere has been a prominent and influential point of reference. Its proponents tend for the most part to talk in optimistic terms about Britain's prospects after Brexit and have effectively framed sceptics and 'Remoaners' as doom-mongers and faint-hearts, ready to talk Britain down.

In substantive terms, May aligned herself with these views by committing the British government to leaving the EU Single Market and Customs Union and the jurisdiction of the European Court of Justice. This is a harder version of Brexit than many mainstream politicians considered plausible or sensible during the referendum debate, although parts of it could be inferred from the campaign positions adopted by Vote Leave. If implemented, it would mean that Britain would set its own tariff rates on goods and services – a longstanding political ambition of Anglo-spherist heirs to the global free trade tradition – but at a likely cost to its trade with the EU. Even at the height of the British Empire in the Edwardian era, Britain's largest export market was the European continent; its 'worldwide pattern of commerce … depended on the capacity of Europe, and particularly of Western Europe, to take the lion's share of its higher value added exports.'[12]

A gaggle of economists and Conservative politicians have taken the view that the UK should adopt an even more trenchant approach than this in its negotiations with the EU and be ready and willing to walk away from them, without agreeing a deal, if the terms offered by their EU counterparts are overly harsh. This idea – the so-called WTO option – was not supported by any mainstream politician or commentator during the campaign itself, but it gathered momentum on parts of the political right, with some insisting that the best option for the UK would not necessarily be to agree an encompassing free trade deal with the EU.[13] The Conservative party manifesto for the 2017 general election repeated this claim, asserting that 'no deal is better than a bad deal', even though this stance has almost no support from the business sector, the trade unions, academic experts or foreign governments. The inconclusive result of this election, and the humiliating rebuff it delivered to May, seriously weakened support for it in parliament.

Yet the sense that an alternative geo-political and eco-nomic pathway lies ready and waiting for the UK, in the form of the Anglosphere, has worked its way into the mainstream of British politics since 2016. It has come to acquire particular salience as some of the political figures most closely associated with it – including Boris Johnson, David Davis and Liam Fox – assumed senior positions in the cabinet appointed by the new prime minister in 2016 and were reappointed to these roles after the general election of 2017. Johnson, as foreign secretary, attempted to revive the idea – abandoned since the late 1960s – of Britain as a significant military presence 'east of Suez'. In a keynote speech delivered in Bahrain in December 2016, he declared this ambition on the basis that the UK was opening a naval support facility there, creating a permanent army presence in Oman, and establishing new defence staff centres in Dubai and Singapore.[14] What struck most experts was the scale of the mismatch between this imperial-era rhetoric and the reality of the UK's diminishing military capability. It now has only one surviving army garrison in Asia, which is funded by the Sultan in Brunei.

Since the referendum, the habit of referencing Anglophone countries as potentially important trading partners, and closer allies, has become much more pronounced, and the EU and its constituent countries have – for the time being – become more distant in imaginative terms. In these emergent and often poorly evidenced arguments about trade and political community, considerations of geographical proximity have increasingly lost out to those of history and heritage. One of the key pieces of evidence for such claims is that, in the past decade, Britain's exports to Commonwealth countries have risen far faster than those to EU countries. Indeed, while exports to the Commonwealth have shown very strong growth, those to the EU may have actually been contracting.[15] And yet, in total, Commonwealth countries account for a relatively small share of UK exports – somewhere between 6 per cent and 8 per cent during the past two decades. By contrast, the EU accounts for almost half of all of UK's exports. The much-cited relative decline of the EU as a trading partner is in truth more a result of the rise of China than the growing importance of the Commonwealth. Just as importantly, the UK has been an integral part of the EU supply chain in sectors such as car manufacturing, aerospace and machinery industries in a way that has no parallel in its relations with Commonwealth countries. When it comes to trade, it seems that 'geography trumps history' decisively.[16]

And yet the ideas underpinning these hopes have worked their way into the political ether and remain potent. One instance of this turn in public discourse is the prevalence of the phrase 'Global Britain', a shorthand for those seeking to pitch Brexit as a choice between a narrow and partial loyalty to a failing EU and a more expansive geo-political and economic outlook. The latter has to a considerable degree been imagined in terms associated with the Anglosphere. The potentially retrogressive aspects of this discursive shift remain the subject of considerable political debate, with many liberals concerned at what may constitute a powerful current of nostalgia for the era of empire. Media reports that, shortly before Liam Fox attended a meeting of Commonwealth trade ministers, civil servants had taken to referring – in satirical terms – to Brexit as 'Empire 2.0' provoked embarrassed and angry responses from ministers. But, despite these denials, Brexit has created the opportunity for the resurrection of forms of national nostalgia which have been marginal or taboo in British politics since the 1950s. Some of the signature policy ideas associated with leaving the EU are telling in this regard. These include the announcement that the traditional blue passport associated with British citizenship would soon be replacing the EU's red model. Other ideas floated in the aftermath of the referendum include a dedicated channel for visitors from the Commonwealth at the UK border.

But the notion of 'Empire 2.0' can distract from the specific character and contemporary appeal of the ideological project that notions of the Anglosphere have most effectively aided in recent years. It is advocates of a free market, neo-liberal future for the UK who remain its most enthusiastic champions. As one investment analyst recently observed of the Anglosphere countries: 'They have generally pro-business economic systems that have secured a high degree of prosperity for their citizens ... The Anglosphere, including America, accounts for more than one-quarter of the world's GDP. The vast majority of the world's leading software, biotechnology, and aerospace firms are concentrated in English-speaking countries.'[17] But advocates of the free market Anglosphere also found themselves concerned at the direction taken by the UK government, which, under Theresa May, signalled an interest in returning to the Chamberlainite formula of industrial support and social reform and pivoting away from the liberal political economy favoured by most proponents of the Anglosphere. The growing divergence between a powerful current of economic liberalism and a more nationalistic conservatism has emerged as one of the most entrenched fault lines in Western politics. It surfaced powerfully in the USA and helped propel Donald Trump to victory in the presidential election of 2016. Trump also looks like a considerable potential obstacle to the liberal Anglosphere, not least because of his isolationist rhetoric and tilt towards protectionist policies. Having risen to greater prominence than it has enjoyed for a century, the Anglosphere is once more faced with formidable, and perhaps insurmountable, political obstacles.

But while Trump may represent the negation of the liberal parts of this heritage, his accession also signals the renewal of an older version of Anglo-America which reaches back to the ethno-nationalism associated with the Anglo-Saxonist movement of the 1890s, and which regards both countries as linked by their shared ethnic and cultural origins. This, broadly, is the outlook promoted by the influential alt-right website Breitbart News and advanced by Trump's former chief strategist Steve Bannon. It coheres around support for stronger immigration controls, an aggressively anti-Muslim form of identity politics and greater protectionism for the jobs of the indigenous working class. Writing on the Breitbart site in 2016, James Pinkerton elaborated this position, invoking the Anglosphere as a potential alliance upon which an anti-Islamic Western order could be rebuilt.[18] And, according to the former UKIP advisor (and one-time editor-in-chief of Breitbart News London) Raheem Kassam,

'The whole Breitbart thing and the whole Trump narrative is about the Anglosphere, about free trade agreements
with all the English speaking nations of the world. That's
the game.'[19]

For proponents of this outlook, including Trump, the
EU's perceived inability to deal with the rising threat of
political Islamic radicalism was the primary justification
for Brexit. For Trump, this has made the UK an important
point of reference, a conviction reinforced by some of his
advisors' links with Nigel Farage and other British Eurosceptics. More generally, the political and corporate networks which the new president has assiduously cultivated
are transatlantic in character and outlook and emanate
from a longstanding set of networks and institutions which
have often been committed to the ideals of the Anglosphere. These include such organisations as the Heritage
Foundation, the Charles G. Koch Foundation, the Cato
Institute and the (now disbanded) Atlantic Bridge.

Longstanding proponents of the Anglosphere are typically sceptical or ambivalent about Trump, but some are
convinced that the time is now ripe for a decisive move
towards the reunification of the English-speaking peoples.
This is the firm belief of James Bennett, who, as we have
seen, has been a consistent proponent of this outlook for
over two decades. In recent writings he offers support for
a new variant of the Anglosphere which has gained salience
since Brexit. This is 'CANZUK', a proposed union of
Canada, Australia, New Zealand and the UK, which he
regards as a first step towards alliance with other Anglophone states, such as India and Singapore. For Bennett,
and others such as the British Conservative writer Andrew
Roberts,[20] what makes this step both plausible and attractive is the unusually high degree of trust that exists between
them – as illustrated by the 'Five Eyes' intelligence-sharing
arrangement. Such an alliance creates the potential for
these states to respond to the rising cost of advanced weap-
onry and their own straightened public finances by pooling
their capabilities.

The vision associated with hypothetical arrangements such as CANZUK goes some way beyond trade deals: 'In international trade talk, and especially in the European context, the ideal for which the parties are striving are the four flows: of goods and services, people, capital, and information.'[21] Bennett's conviction, and that of other proponents of this view, is that some of the constitutive features of the EU can now be more successfully re-created in this geographically dispersed, but culturally contiguous, alliance of Anglophone countries, including the creation of a unified military and an overarching political authority. In such accounts there is no trace of the anxieties about sovereignty and control which bubbled to the surface of British political culture in relation to the EU. Instead, the prevalent assumption is that, by turning back to the old dominion countries and the USA, the British are coming home.

Bennett is sufficiently realistic to note that the current turn to control inward immigration may well put an obstacle in the way of a union that seeks to promote the free movement of peoples, but he is confident too that the case for preferential arrangements among the peoples of these states would be a popular one on the basis of their historical ties. He has recently floated the possibility that, as the UK becomes ever more crowded, it might envisage a programme of mass emigration to the spacious parts of the old Commonwealth – an argument that offers an unnerving reprise of Britain's settler colonialist past.

Newer voices in the UK have been drawn to a similar position. According to the *Daily Telegraph* columnist and Brexiteer economist Andrew Lilico, a new free trade deal between some of the leading English-speaking countries may well smooth the path towards the establishment of greater military cooperation between them.[22] Like Bennett, he takes the emergence of new forms of technological innovation to signal a paradigmatic shift which means that countries such as the UK can now trade just as effectively with far-flung states as with neighbours. The arrival of the

internet is seen by some advocates of this view as a vehicle
for the increasing promulgation of the English language.
For Victor Hill, 'English is the language of the internet and
it is the English-speaking countries which have adapted to
the information economy most enthusiastically ... But if
English is the language of the internet, it is because it is
also the language of science.'[23]

Among these proponents, there is a recurrent interest in
detecting signs of support for such a prospect in other
Anglophone countries, but in practice the same handful of
figures elsewhere tend to be offered as evidence of an
uptick of interest in the Anglosphere in its constituent
countries. This is an idea that has been appropriated and
recycled in conservative circles elsewhere. Most recently,
Jason Kenney, MP for Calgary, a former minister and
future Conservative leadership candidate, suggested that
'A post Brexit UK should go to the front of the queue for
a free trade agreement with Canada.'[24] And several candi-
dates for the leadership of the Conservative Party of
Canada indicated their strong support for the CANZUK
idea in 2017.

Whether these calls reflect a growing interest in this
prospect in Canada in particular is an open question. In
the era of Trump and May, the liberal vision of the insti-
tutionalised Anglosphere still looks as unlikely as it did
during the era of the UK's membership of the EU. But now
it plays a slightly different role in the political mainstream,
evoking old dreams and new hopes about where Britain
sits in the world. Such ideas also play a rather different
but no less important political role. They connect with,
and give voice to, the growing divergence of outlooks
among the constituent parts of the United Kingdom. The
Anglosphere and related ideas, such as imperial federation,
have always carried implications for the internal organisation of the UK itself. As we showed in chapter 1, federal
dreams were never brought to bear upon the internal constitution of the home country, despite various attempts to
do so. And yet, over the course of the last century, the

English character of the Anglosphere has become increasingly prominent, and the emergence of a free market version of it in the last years of the twentieth century has sustained a more distinctly Anglicised vision of politics and economy. This trend has been accentuated too by the introduction of devolution for other parts of the UK and the growing focus upon political forms of English identity (especially since the Scottish referendum of 2014).

In signalling its commitment to radical disentanglement from the EU, including the Single Market and Customs Union, the UK government – now led by a more traditional kind of English Conservative – appears to have set itself on a collision course with Northern Ireland and Scotland, where clear majorities voted for 'Remain'. In these contexts, supple and delicate kinds of statecraft, and a willingness to compromise and broker new deals, may well now be required, rather than the kind of high-handed Unionism which has at earlier historical moments resulted in damaging losses to the territorial integrity of the UK.

In Scotland, the SNP government will seize the chance to present a future deal as uniquely damaging to Scotland. And in Northern Ireland, the potential re-emergence of a 'hard' border between the Republic and the North could have significant, destabilising consequences in both security and economic terms. The preponderantly English tones of the Anglosphere have been brought to the surface by Brexit and the campaign to regain sovereignty from the EU. But a moment of existential choice may well lie ahead for its advocates. Do they wish to pursue this agenda within the asymmetrical structures and difficult compromises which the maintenance of the United Kingdom now requires, or will they seek to re-create Greater Britain by releasing England from its shackles?

Conclusion

For many critics, both inside and outside the UK, the idea of 'Global Britain' breaking free from the shackles of the EU to resume its buccaneering, free-trading heritage is a dangerous, nostalgic delusion. There is certainly a good chance that leaving the EU's Customs Union and the Single Market, in the name of resuming the freedom associated with a global trading role, will result in significant economic dislocation and the loss of geo-political influence for the UK. Yet such considerations do not persuade adherents of the Anglosphere, for whom the desire to leave the EU stems from powerful sentiments about the idea of a reclaimed sovereignty and the renewal of historical connections with 'Anglo-world' societies. We have sought to show, in the preceding chapters of this book, that the lineage of thought and sentiment that has given shape to this ideal – running for more than a century from the era of Greater Britain though to Brexit – is both fluid and evolving and affords a bounty of motifs, images and ideas that have been continually reworked and redeployed in high politics.

There is more to the endurance of the notions of Greater Britain, the British Commonwealth or the more recently

coined Anglosphere, we suggest, than a stubborn or mis-
informed refusal to countenance the loss of empire. They
evoke a broad and fluid stream of thinking which has different tributaries and occasionally flows in different political directions. But while this thinking is intimately bound
up in arguments about Britain's imperial reach, and its
roots go back to debates about the relationship between
the North American settler colonies and the Crown-in-
Parliament that took place during the 'First British Empire'
of the eighteenth century, it has been utilised within a
range of political discourses and projects. It coalesced in
the late Victorian era at the conjunction of ideas about
England's civilisational influence and geo-political emi-
nence and new currents of Anglo-Saxonist theorising.
These discourses were subsequently mobilised in support
of Chamberlain's audacious attempt to align the class
interests of British industrialists and their workers in a new
political economy of empire and to justify a system of
imperial preference, a position that represented a significant break from the established orthodoxies of economic
liberalism. And, while Chamberlain's project was defeated,
it created the space for new arguments in favour of imperial unity and greater economic self-reliance as the British
Empire was stretched to its limits by the First World War
and the world economic depression of the 1930s.

Victory for Britain in the global conflict that broke out
in 1939 came at great cost and created the conditions for
the UK's continued relative economic decline in the decades
that followed. The rise of the USA to global pre-eminence
was now complete, the end of empire a foregone conclu-
sion, and Europe deeply divided between its Western and
Eastern parts. These powerful dynamics formed the backdrop to Churchill's attempt to reinvent the Anglosphere
as an alliance of English-speaking peoples that could offer
new cultural and political leadership to Europe in particular and the newly minted 'West' more generally. Some
of the notable ambiguities contained within Churchill's
vision – for instance over Europe – and the political and

economic costs associated with this framework led large parts of Britain's political establishment to conclude that joining the new, dynamic Western European market on the UK's doorstep was now in the national interest. This judgement also reflected a diminishing faith in the economic value of the Commonwealth alliance. The UK's engagement with Europe was framed in both prudential and instrumental terms from the outset. European membership was never underpinned by deep popular support or real affective sentiment. And the shallowness of its roots in British culture and society would ultimately aid the demise of the idea of the UK as a committed European power. The Anglosphere, by contrast, still packed a sentimental punch, feeling to many like a more authentic source of belonging for Britain, an idea that was increasingly harnessed by those determined to pull Britain out of the EU.

But while the Anglosphere was appropriated and reinvented throughout the twentieth century, there were limits to the range of political visions and ideas to which it could be harnessed. This is a deeply embedded lineage that carries powerful historical connotations and long cultural associations. It has also been enabled and conditioned by Britain's political economy in different eras. Late Victorian ideas of Greater Britain and imperial federation became meaningful in the context of the massive flows of trade, investment and peoples between the United Kingdom and her settler dominions, as well as the exercise of imperial state power, which ranged from the everyday and mundane to the brutal use of military force to subjugate and repress colonial populations.[1] Anglosphere ideas were also closely attuned to, and informed by, the emergence of new technologies and practices, including the development of railways and telegrams, advances in agricultural production and food storage, an Anglo-world cultural economy of household consumption and media outlets, new military structures and institutions, and the development of imperial forms of state administration.

Lingering tensions within this political economy between the interests of different social classes and sectors burst into the open in debates about tariff reform. Chamberlain's reworking of the Greater Britain ideal foundered, politically, on the rocks of Gladstonian liberalism – specifically the goals of 'free trade, sound money and a balanced budget',[2] which continued to haunt British policy-makers over the next century. But his ideas enjoyed a new lease of life as they won further support in the 1930s, when his political successors crafted an imperial protectionist, cheap money response to the global depression of those years. And so, even as the dominions edged ever closer to complete independence from the mother country, new trade flows, the development of mass popular culture and strong military alliances meant that it was still feasible to endow the Anglosphere dream with a new lease of political life.

Nearly bankrupted by the Second World War, Britain turned – in both economic and imaginative terms – back to the 'Old Commonwealth' and her remaining colonies to underpin her economic revival and the financing of the newly created welfare state. It did so within the new conditions created by the USA after the war, including a global economy governed by Bretton Woods institutions. But, following the debacle of Suez in 1956, repeated currency crises, and the drift into relative economic decline, Britain's political establishment looked for new solutions and so came to seek entry to the EEC. Now, the Anglosphere came to play a very different role in British political culture. It enabled the expression of powerful forms of guilt, nostalgia and anti-European prejudice – as much on the political left as on the right – in the form of support for the Commonwealth. Henceforth, Britain would deepen its economic and political engagement with Europe, and the latter began to pursue deeper and wider forms of legal and political integration. From the 1960s onwards, Canada, Australia and New Zealand were all turning to form regional partnerships of their own. By 1979, the Anglo-world appeared to be no more.

But, in the 1980s and 1990s, during and after the premiership of Margaret Thatcher, the Anglosphere ideal became salient and meaningful once more. Its re-emergence was enabled and conditioned by a combination of factors, most notably a new wave of economic globalisation, the rise of a new, financialised form of capitalism, the end of the Cold War, growing disaffection with the EU, and the widespread diffusion of new technologies of information and mass communication. Together, these dynamics created the conditions in which questions of belonging and nationhood returned to the fore in politics and were felt in different ways across the territories of the UK. This created an opening for the Anglosphere to be taken off the historical shelf, dusted down, suitably remodelled, and presented as an attractive garb for a new current of free market Euroscepticism that was mustering on the fringes of British politics.

Such a vision made more sense in a context where the world economy was still dominated by the United States, but the main sources of dynamism within it were now domiciled in Asia, not Europe. At the same time, the City of London was once more assuming global pre-eminence as a centre of finance capital. Important new communications technologies were being developed in the USA, and these came to underpin new forms of global trade and connection. Europe appeared diminished both as a site of economic dynamism and innovation and as a power within world politics. For the UK, it was no longer the central theatre for British security interests, nor was it the pole of cultural and intellectual attraction that it had been in the 1960s and 1970s.

This gradual fall in Europe's 'output legitimacy' was accelerated by the global financial crisis of 2007–8 and its aftermath. The crisis in the eurozone dragged on for years, leading to prolonged stagnation and mass unemployment in a number of the EU's debtor member states. By contrast, Canada and Australia escaped the worst of the global recession, while the USA, under Obama, relaxed its fiscal policy to restore growth. China also embarked on a huge credit-led stimulus. These moves created the perfect economic and political storm for those arguing the case for a major shift of orientation on the UK's part, away from Europe. Increasingly it was argued that Asia and the Anglosphere represented the future of the world economy and Europe its past. A unique, unprecedented opportunity to pitch these arguments to the British electorate was afforded by David Cameron's decision to offer a referendum in order to shore up his own position within the Conservative Party during its years of coalition government after 2010.

Presented in its baldest terms, a neo-Thatcherite idea of Brexit, which involves stripping away tariff barriers, reducing labour market and product regulations, and trading at 'world prices' remains a potentially toxic position to present to a public weary of austerity, facing years of declining living standards, and increasingly jaded in the face of the economic liberalism associated with the last few decades of government. But this vision has been rendered considerably more palatable, and given a patina of historical depth, when presented through the narrative and ethos of the English-speaking peoples. Its deployment has supplied a new way of reimagining Britain's role in the world and affords a rich repository of motifs, images and emotional resources to give narrative structure and symbolic content to a neo-liberal species of Euroscepticism.

And there is much for pundits and politicians of this dispensation to plunder when they turn in this direction. There is the English language itself, the *lingua franca* of global finance. There are the commemorative rituals of shared military struggle in world wars, which have proved so powerful in constituting the national identities of Canada, Australia and New Zealand, as well as Great Britain. And there are popular cultural resources drawn from the media, sport, travel, and the histories and experiences of millions of families.

In telling this important but neglected story, we have placed quite considerable emphasis on the contingencies and contexts associated with the changing political land-scape. But we have also highlighted some of the longer-running dynamics shaping the UK's political economy and pointed to some of the continuous aspects of the Anglo-sphere lineage. One powerful recurrent trope closely asso-ciated with it is the notion of Britain as a maritime 'world island', ruling the waves in the realm of commerce, and with a pedigree as one of the world's great naval powers. This particular idea runs like a gossamer thread through the discursive history of the Anglosphere, linking Seeley to Churchill and today's cheerleaders for 'Global Britain'. Maritime imagery speaks particularly to familiar ideas about Britain's history and to the enduring notion of its fundamental identity as a seafaring nation. It is typically endowed with distinctly entrepreneurial attributes. One Anglosphere enthusiast has recently enlisted Sir Francis Drake as an ancestral symbol for the buccaneering global entrepreneurs who will be liberated by Brexit from the shackles of Brussels bureaucracy.[3] These images rehearse well-worn depictions of the English as an island people, a providential nation which nurtured the oak of British liberty, from which there have grown the branches of democracy, the rule of law and the free market economy, inventions that have been replanted across the English-speaking parts of the world.

Other notable recurrent features of this discourse include its ingrained tendency – like other powerful forms of national imaginary – to gain purchase and meaning from that which it is defined against. As a geo-political point of reference, the Anglosphere has typically been defined in relation to other constellations and alliances in the world, and this remains an important aspect of its appeal and operation. The founding vision of this lineage – Seeley's idea of the expansion of England – was informed by its author's premonition of a world in which Greater Britain would compete with the two great powers emerging in global politics, the USA and Russia. For Churchill, from 1943, up to Thatcher, it was the communist East that provided the menace against which the idea of a Western order shaped around the values and political economy of Anglo-America acquired meaning. In more recent times, the weakening economies of Southern Europe and an apparently unaccountable EU state provided handy foils for the expression of the Anglosphere dream.

But the Anglosphere idea is not defined merely by that which it opposes. It also reflects a deep-rooted sense of cultural commitment and civilisational vision, and it has always been anchored by strong beliefs – which have altered across different eras – about who belongs most authentically to it and who does not. In the later Victorian era, widely shared notions of racial hierarchy seeped into an outlook which assumed that the indigenous peoples of the settler dominions lacked the capacity and rights that were natural possessions of the civilised English colonists who moved to their lands (unless they were simply too strong, like the Maori, to be forcibly subjugated). There were always important gradations of difference within this widely shared sense of racial hierarchy, and difficult cases to grapple with. White non-English speaking peoples, who settled lands along with Anglophone equivalents, presented one set of problems, for instance in French-speaking Canada. Other peoples, notably the Boers in South Africa, who possessed a providential sense of their own distinctiveness posed different kinds of difficulty for the guardians of empire. India has always proved problematic for Anglosphere theorists, from Seeley onwards. Its population size and sheer diversity meant that it could not be assimilated to political or racial arguments deployed for unity with the settler colonies. It consistently resisted imperialism and eventually threw off both the British Empire and its monarchy.[4] For other reasons – religious difference and resistance to British rule among them – Southern Ireland could never be securely embraced in the Anglosphere imagination, which the Republic's continued membership of the EU, as the UK heads to leave it, now serves only to reinforce.

After 1945, rising numbers of Commonwealth migrants into the UK also began to raise profound, and often difficult, questions about the ethnic and cultural make-up of the British, and a powerful counter-current of popular racism took hold. Most recently, in the wake of the 2016 referendum result, the presence of 2.9 million EU nationals in the country became a matter of significant political contention, bringing the question of who belongs in the 'home' of the English-speaking peoples back to the fore.

But as the UK struggles to agree a deal on Brexit with the EU and is required to deal with a raft of complex choices in trade, security, the environment and immigration in its negotiations with its former EU partners, the question of whom the UK now sides with, and whom it does not, looms very large. Faced by a more isolationist USA, led currently by a highly unpredictable president, and with the EU as a key bulwark against an increasingly assertive Russia and a close partner in attempts to combat terrorism, the task of drawing clear lines around allies and foes looks increasingly fraught for the UK. The Anglosphere offers one response to this dilemma, but, given the lack of enthusiasm for it in the political cultures of the other countries it references, and the fact that geographic proximity matters more than sentiment in determining trade flows, it cannot provide realistic solutions or long-term comfort.

Equally, as we have illustrated, the Anglosphere is a project that reflects and generates arguments about the internal arrangement of the UK's constituent territories, as well as having a bearing upon its potential external alliances and relationships. In the last three decades in particular, its advocacy has become entangled with the development of a more self-consciously 'English' perspective upon the UK. It is notable that the Anglosphere idea appeals for the most part to Conservatives who adhere to a liberal political economy and a cultural individualism which is more strongly embedded in Southern England than other parts of the UK, and this divergence has been accentuated by the provision of devolution for all of its non-English countries. This is not a simple or clear-cut process. There are numerous people in Scotland, Wales and Northern Ireland, for instance, with strong ties in other parts of the Commonwealth. But the renewed enthusiasm for the Anglosphere is intimately intertwined with a growing sense of English national consciousness, which as yet lacks clear institutional recognition. As a distinctively 'Anglo' imaginary has crystallised over the last thirty years, at some remove from the institutions and ethos of the British systems of politics and government, the outward-looking Anglosphere ideal has become a particularly appealing national frame for a significant group of Conservative politicians.

The scholarly understanding of the reception of the Anglosphere idea among different audiences remains rather limited. The bulk of the academic discussion of the concept has focused upon the supply of ideas about it and the main authors of these. While there is a prevalent assumption that younger people are more invested in the European idea, it appears that the right of free movement between the Anglosphere countries is also popular with this cohort, and indeed that empire is still viewed fairly positively in large parts of British society.[5] There are different cultural and family connections with these countries at work across the UK, and these have helped ensure that this discourse has some traction at a more popular level.

But the context in which such ideas are propagated has altered profoundly. The Anglosphere is now being invoked at a point when a remorseless shift of power and influence away from the West is under way. Historically it is an idea that came to the fore during the era of Western domination and leadership in world affairs. Its lofty civilisational ambitions, celebration of representative government and free market orientation make much less sense in the world that is now emerging.

It seems likely, though, that it will remain a pertinent and recurrent point of reference in the UK, partly because of its association with Brexit, but also since it is so deeply embedded in the political and institutional cultures of the state. In historical terms, the Anglosphere lineage has been reflected on all parts of the political spectrum and has gained supporters among progressive leaders and intellectuals, as well as their counterparts on the right. In the early part of the twentieth century, leading Fabian figures supported social imperialism, and the Labour Party was led by figures who believed strongly in empire. And after 1945, even when Labour politicians supported decolonisation and the economic aspirations of developing countries, deep personal attachments to the 'Old Commonwealth' persisted for figures such as Gaitskell and Wilson. These associations contributed to a marked ambivalence about the UK's membership of the fledgling EEC in the 1960s and 1970s and formed one ingredient within the more visceral Euroscepticism of the party's left. Only in the 1980s did Labour move towards a more securely pro-European position, but this did not mean that these older allegiances entirely fell away. In fact, both Anglo-American and Anglosphere ties informed the argument for a 'Third Way' in New Labour circles, an ideology that appeared to fuse both European and Anglophone elements. Tony Blair himself inhabited at least two of Churchill's three circles at any one time.

The vote for Brexit in 2016 reopened divisions in Labour circles which had been sidestepped for thirty years. Labour went into the 2017 election fudging its stance on the key issues of whether it advocated leaving the Single Market or not. The wider question which the party will face after Brexit is where it will turn for inspiration and identification when the UK is out of the EU. What will the left have to say about Britain's place in the world and its relations with other Anglophone countries, and can it craft an international vision which does not draw from the well of Euroscepticism or rely upon fantasies about 'Global Britain'?

Answers to these questions remain hard to imagine, in part because the Anglosphere heritage has been most prominently and confidently claimed by some British Conservatives and their allies rather than by the Labour Party and the liberal left. Chamberlain's liberal unionists allied themselves to Tory imperialists who were prepared to break with the pieties of free trade. They developed a potent fusion of British patriotism, colonial racism, a protectionist approach to trade, and a more interventionist political economy that was designed to redress the balance between finance and industrial capital. While this project failed under Chamberlain's leadership, aspects of it were incorporated in the approach taken by the National governments of the 1930s. After the Second World War, the Conservative heirs of this tradition sought to promote the idea of special alliances with the 'Old Commonwealth', but most Tories came to accept arguments for European integration and the broadly Keynesian consensus about economic policy. Indeed a combination of pro-European, 'One Nation' and economic-liberal values coalesced as the dominant perspective within the Conservative Party during the 1960s and 1970s. Its champion Ted Heath passed this mantle on to later figures such as Michael Heseltine and Kenneth Clarke.

But, in the early years of the twenty-first century, this line has all but disappeared, mainly due to the profound impact of Margaret Thatcher upon British Conservative politics. In her shadow the Anglosphere was now invoked by a small number of Conservatives who wanted to yoke Euroscepticism to the Gladstonian tradition of free trade, sound money and a small state, jettisoning the residual interventionism of the One Nation tradition. The EU remained the source of considerable disagreement on the political right, with many Conservative MPs supporting the idea of remaining within it for prudential economic reasons, but also with a large number siding with the Leave position. Following the selection of Theresa May as prime minister, some of the tensions associated with these different lines of thought were brought to the surface once more. In office from June 2016, she invoked the 'Global

Britain' of the neo-liberals while reaching back to the Chamberlainite tradition of social reform and industrial intervention. This was a rather incoherent fusion, which was poorly presented and lacked policy coherence, and it crashed on the rocks of the election that May chose to fight in 2017.

These political considerations aside, the revival of interest in the Anglosphere in recent years represents an attempt not just to alter policy and politics but, more fundamentally, to reimagine English – and indeed British – history; to reconstruct a national historiography for a time when the UK has left the European Union. As the celebrated historian J. G. A. Pocock argued in the early 1990s, if the key to Anglo-British history was 'the maintenance of a sovereign structure over four centuries', then the pooling of sovereignty in the EU necessitated the reworking of that history to produce new historiographical reflections on Britain as a European power (as well as an extension of European history to embrace the British Isles).[6] Withdrawal from the EU would appear to entail the opposite: a renewed attempt to write the history of England back into a world-island lineage, with sovereignty at its core. This is what is represented by the recent interest in the idea of the Anglosphere – and the histories of the British Empire penned by Niall Ferguson and others that have accompanied it. It is therefore no surprise that the re-emergence of this old perspective upon Britain and its place in the world has triggered a new round of 'history wars' among scholarly experts and public historians, all engaged in the task of telling and contesting the national story at a moment of dislocation and profound uncertainty.

Pocock's insistence on the centrality of sovereignty in Anglo-British history touches on one of the central fault lines in the Anglosphere project. The experience of civil war in the seventeenth century led the English to insist on the importance of the indivisibility of the sovereignty of the Crown-in-Parliament, he maintained. Rather than share sovereignty, they incorporated Scotland and Ireland into their governing structures, and they simply could not 'envisage a sharing of parliamentary sovereignty with the American colonies and, in the end, preferred to let them go if they could not be conquered; the "Empire" of the body politic over itself had higher priority than an Empire of the seas and continents.'[7] A federal solution, which might have accommodated aspirations to self-government in Ireland, the settler colonies or other parts of the British Empire, could not therefore be countenanced, and so schemes for the unity of Greater Britain or the Anglosphere which relied on political federation were doomed. Rejected as unfeasible at Westminster, such ideas were instead exported to Europe and, more problematically still, to the former colonies of the British Empire, such as the West Indies, Central Africa and Malaysia.

The contention at the heart of this book, that the Anglosphere – or, rather, the pattern of thinking associated with it – has been integral to British politics, cuts against the conventional view that the only alternative attachment to the European one, for the British elite, has been the special relationship with the USA. The case for the importance of Anglo-America in British political history has been well made in recent years. Specifically, the notion that a shared understanding of the merits of the liberal market economy, common approaches to social provision and economic policy-making, similar kinds of labour market, and interwoven thinking about policy underpins an Anglo-American political community has been persuasively asserted.

Yet, despite the undoubted existence and importance of this transatlantic community, it is important also to remind ourselves of the multiple attachments and different forms of imagined community which have been at play in British political discourse. Sometimes these have seemed to be complementary and sometimes conflicting. Our overriding aim has been to draw attention to a form of affiliation which has been rather overlooked and is easily obscured by the focus upon Anglo-America. There are good reasons to pick out distinguishing features of the Anglosphere lineage, we suggest. Its roots in the history and thinking of empire, for instance, mean that it has a rich store of memories, fantasies and ideas to draw upon. But it needs emphasis too because of the recurrence of differences of focus and outlook between the USA and other Anglosphere countries, a situation that sometimes created acute dilemmas for Britain. This was certainly true for Churchill during the Second World War, and this tension has resurfaced at key junctures since, most notably during the Iraq War of 2003.

There is, therefore, a good case for bringing the Anglosphere lineage into the foreground of the interpretation of British politics. But, having observed its prominence in the thinking of some of the leading political actors who identified with it and noted the complex lines of argument that have drawn upon it, we conclude by observing its rather paradoxical political record. For, while this lineage has been integral and recurrently meaningful in a way that has not been sufficiently heeded, it is also the case that the Anglosphere has not been successfully realised in political terms. Some of its leading champions – notably Churchill and Thatcher – used it either for political window dressing or to develop *post-facto* rationalisations for decisions or strategies they wished to pursue. Other figures – such as Chamberlain and Powell – who sought to distil radical policy agendas on the basis of some of its key precepts met ultimately with failure. One reason for the latter was the striking persistence of an embedded, influential nexus of economically liberal ideas about trade and a 'realist' statecraft which has required the UK to cultivate various alliances and unions and to adopt a pragmatic approach to its international liaisons.

Failure is likely to be its fate once again if the Anglosphere is offered as the governing framework for post-Brexit Britain. It will not muster the economic partners and geo-political alliances the UK will require once it exits the EU. Deeply enmeshed in the Single Market and the trading relations managed by the EU, the British economy cannot rely upon the hope of the trading partnerships and tariff preferences of yesteryear being reinvented now. And heady rhetoric about 'Global Britain' will not be enough to overcome the practical challenges that Brexit will generate. It is far more likely that the bulk of Britain's trade will become less, not more, 'free' – contrary to what many Brexiteers hope – if the UK leaves the European Single Market and Customs Union. And, given its largely Eurosceptic tenor, the Anglosphere will also tend to divide the UK, territorially and demographically, rather than unite it behind a new sense of shared national purpose. Meanwhile, the other core countries of the Anglosphere show no serious inclination to join the UK in forging new political and economic alliances. They will, most likely, continue to work within existing regional and international institutions and remain indifferent to – or simply perplexed by – calls for some kind of formalised Anglosphere alliance.

Yet, while there are reasons to reject the notion that the Anglosphere could supply a secure platform for the UK in terms of foreign and economic policy, it is also true that it is hard to imagine a coherent alternative trajectory being pursued at present. Should the UK change its mind and not leave the EU, or if it seeks to leave on much 'softer' and more equivocal terms, it is very unlikely that it will commit enthusiastically to the European project and prioritise its neighbours over its global entanglements. It is, we would suggest, far more likely that the UK will attempt to navigate between its European, Anglospheric and wider global commitments, just as it has done for much of its recent history, only now with diminished geo-political influence and standing. The tragedy of the different national orientations that have emerged in British politics after empire – whether pro-European, Anglo-American, Anglospheric or some combination of these – is that none has yet endowed the UK with a compelling, coherent and popular answer to the question of how it should find its way in the wider world.

Notes

Introduction

1 Eric Hobsbawm, *The Age of Extremes: The Short Twentieth Century 1914–1991* (London: Michael Joseph, 1994).

2 Duncan Bell, *The Idea of Greater Britain: Empire and the Future of World Order, 1869–1900* (Princeton, NJ: Princeton University Press, 2007).

3 Srdjan Vucetic, *The Anglosphere: A Genealogy of a Racialized Identity in International Relations* (Stanford, CA: Stanford University Press, 2011).

4 Richard Aldrich and John Kasuku, 'Escaping from American intelligence: culture, ethnocentrism and the Anglosphere', *International Affairs*, 88/5 (2012), pp. 1009–28.

5 Srdjan Vucetic, 'Bound to follow? The Anglosphere and US-led coalitions of the willing, 1950–2001', *European Journal of International Relations*, 17/1 (2011), pp. 27–49.

6 Andrew Gamble, *Between Europe and America: The Future of British Politics* (London: Palgrave Macmillan, 2004); and João Carlos Espada, *The Anglo-American Tradition of Liberty: A View from Europe* (London: Routledge, 2016).

7 Ben Wellings and Helen Baxendale, 'Euroscepticism and the Anglosphere: traditions and dilemmas in contemporary English nationalism', *Journal of Common Market Studies*, 53/1 (2015), pp. 123–39.

8 See, in particular, James C. Bennett, *The Anglosphere Challenge: Why the English-Speaking Nations Will Lead the Way in the Twenty-First Century* (Lanham, MD: Rowman & Littlefield, 2007).

9 Daniel Hannan, *How We Invented Freedom & Why it Matters* (London: Head of Zeus, 2013); and Michael Kenny and Nick Pearce, 'The rise of the Anglosphere: how the right dreamed up a new conservative world order', *New Statesman*, 10 February 2015.

Chapter 1   The Origins of the Anglosphere

1 Terra Walston Joseph, 'Bulwer-Lytton's *The Coming Race* and an Anglo-Saxon global "Greater Britain" ', *Nineteenth Century Contexts*, 37/3 (2016), pp. 233–48.

2 J. R. Seeley, 'The United States of Europe', *Macmillan's Magazine*, 23 (1871), pp. 436–48 [lecture to the Peace Society].

3 J. R. Seeley, *The Expansion of England* (Chicago: University of Chicago Press, 1971), p. 126.

4 Ibid., p. 227.

5 Ibid., p. 185.

6 Marilyn Lake and Henry Reynolds, *The Global Colour Line: White Men's Countries and the International Challenge of Racial Equality* (Cambridge: Cambridge University Press, 2011).

7 James Belich, *Replenishing the Earth: The Settler Revolution and the Rise of the Anglo-World* (Oxford: Oxford University Press, 2009), p. 49.

8 John Darwin, *The Empire Project: The Rise and Fall of the British World System 1830–1970* (Cambridge: Cambridge University Press, 2009).

9 Belich, *Replenishing the Earth*, p. 4 – not including subject peoples of the British Empire.

10 Ibid., p. 126.

11 Gary B. Magee and Andrew S. Thompson, *Empire and Globalisation* (Cambridge: Cambridge University Press, 2010), pp. 68–72.

12 Belich, *Replenishing the Earth*, pp. 107–8.

13 Ibid., p. 126.

14 Gary Magee, M. Ishaq Bhatti and Alice Shuaishuai Li, 'The economic modeling of migration and consumption patterns in the English-speaking world', *Economic Modelling*, 50 (2015), pp. 322–30.

15 Ged Martin, 'Empire federalism and imperial parliamentary union, 1820–1870', *Historical Journal*, 16/1 (1973), pp. 65–92.

16 Bell, *The Idea of Greater Britain*, p. 13.

17 Edward A. Freeman, *The Growth of the English Constitution from the Earliest Times* (London: Macmillan, 1872), pp. 18–19.

18 See Duncan Bell, *Reordering the World: Essays on Liberalism and Empire* (Princeton, NJ: Princeton University Press, 2016), pp. 321–40.

19 Charles Dilke, cited in Bell, *The Idea of Greater Britain*, p. 117.

20 Cited ibid., p. 115. Froude is said to have referred in private to the 'extermination of Zulus and Kaffirs' who threatened to kill their white rulers.

21 James Bryce, *American Commonwealth* (Indianapolis: Liberty Fund, 2012).

22 Cited in Bell, *The Idea of Greater Britain*, p. 237.

23 Magee and Thompson, *Empire and Globalisation*, p. 173.

24 Cecil Rhodes, 'Confession of faith' (1877), in John E. Flint, *Cecil Rhodes* (Boston: Little, Brown, 1974), pp. 248–52.

25 See Bell, *The Idea of Greater Britain*, pp. 256–7, and Daniel Deudney, 'Greater Britain or greater synthesis? Seeley, Mackinder, and Wells on Britain in the global industrial era', *Review of International Studies*, 27/2 (2001), pp. 187–208.

26 Goldwin Smith, *Canada and the Canadian Question* (1891), cited in Bell, *The Idea of Greater Britain*, p. 255.

27 Smith, cited in Lake and Reynolds, *The Global Colour Line*, pp. 54–5.

28 Duncan Bell, 'Race, utopia, perpetual peace: Andrew Carnegie's dreamworld', in Jean-François Drolet and James Dunkerley (eds), *American Foreign Policy: Studies in Intellectual History* (Manchester: Manchester University Press, 2017).

29 Vucetic, *The Anglosphere*.

30 Theodore Roosevelt, Fourth Annual Message to Congress, 6 December 1904, www.presidency.ucsb.edu/ws/?pid=29545.

31 Adam Tooze, *The Deluge: The Great War and the Remaking of Global Order* (London: Allen Lane, 2014), p. 401.

32 Eric Hobsbawm, *The Age of Empire* (London: Abacus, 1987), p. 51.

33 Enoch Powell, *Joseph Chamberlain* (London: Thames & Hudson, 1977), p. 52.

34 Ibid., p. 72.

35 Peter Clarke, *Hope and Glory: Britain 1900–2000* (2nd edn, London: Penguin, 2004), pp. 26–7.

36 E. H. H. Green, 'The political economy of empire', in A. Porter (ed.), *The Oxford History of the British Empire*, Vol. III: *The Nineteenth Century* (Oxford University Press, 1999), p. 361.

37 Cited in Walter Nimocks, *Milner's Young Men: The 'Kindergarten' in Edwardian Imperial Affairs* (Durham, NC: Duke University Press, 1968), p. 130.

38 Minutes of Round Table meeting, 15–18 January 1910, Lothian Papers, cited in Alex May, 'The Round Table and imperial federation, 1910–17', *The Round Table*, 99/410 (2010), pp. 547–56.

39 The situation in South Africa at the outbreak of war was more complicated. Afrikaners rebelled against conscription in October 1914 to fight the German colony of South-West Africa and were put down by the union government of Louis Botha.

40 Clarke, *Hope and Glory*, p. 102.

41 Lake and Reynolds, *The Global Colour Line*, p. 146.

42 Belich, *Replenishing the Earth*, p. 471.

43 Ibid., p. 472.

44 John Darwin, *Unfinished Empire: The Global Expansion of Britain* (London: Penguin, 2013), p. 339.

45 Cited in Lionel Curtis, *World War, its Cause and Cure* (2nd edn, London: Oxford University Press, 1945), p. 34.

46 Lothian's efforts to secure America's support in the Second World War led Churchill to describe him as Britain's 'greatest ambassador to the United States', rescuing his reputation for posterity after he had advocated appeasement and made two notorious visits to Hitler in the 1930s.

47 Curtis, *World War, its Cause and Cure*, p. 110.

Chapter 2   After Empire

1 Winston Churchill, *A History of the English-Speaking Peoples* (London: Folio Society, 2002).
2 See, for instance, Daniel Hannan, *How We Invented Freedom and Why it Matters* (London: Head of Zeus, 2013).
3 Srdjan Vucetic, *The Anglosphere: A Genealogy of a Racialized Identity in International Relations* (Stanford, CA: Stanford University Press, 2011).
4 William Roger Louis, *Speak for England: Leo Amery and the British Empire in the Age of Churchill* (London: I. B. Tauris, 2013).
5 Richard Toye, *Churchill's Empire: The World that Made Him and the World he Made* (Basingstoke: Macmillan, 2015).
6 'The "half-naked", "seditious fakir", *Mahatma Gandhi's Writings, Philosophy, Audio, Video and Photographs*, www.mkgandhi.org/students/thiswasbapu/144halfnakedfakir.htm.
7 Churchill's role in the Bengal famine of 1943 has long been the subject of considerable historical controversy and has been raised most recently by Shashi Tharoor, in 'The ugly Briton', *Time*, 29 November 2010; http://content.time.com/time/magazine/article/0,9171,2031992,00.html.
8 Peter Clarke, *The Locomotive of War: Money, Power, Empire and Guilt* (London: Bloomsbury, 2017).
9 Chris Schoeman, *Churchill's South Africa: Travels during the Anglo-Boer War* (London: Zebra Press, 2014).
10 Carroll Kilpatrick, Mahan's foremost disciples, *VQR: A National Journal of Literature & Discussion*, 93/3 (2017), www.vqronline.org/mahan%E2%80%99s-foremost-disciples.
11 For a balanced discussion of his subsequently notorious views, see Toye, *Churchill's Empire*, p. 145.
12 John Ramsden, *Man of the Century: Winston Churchill and the Legend since 1945* (London: HarperCollins, 2002); and John Charmley, *Churchill: The End of Glory* (London: Hodder & Stoughton, 1993).
13 Christopher Hitchens, *Blood, Class and Nostalgia: Anglo-American Ironies* (London: Vintage, 1991), pp. 203–4.
14 Benn Steil, *The Battle of Bretton Woods: John Maynard Keynes, Harry Dexter White, and the Making of a New*

World Order (Princeton, NJ: Princeton University Press, 2014), p. 332.

15 John Darwin, *The Empire Project* (Cambridge: Cambridge University Press, 2011).

16 Charmley, *Churchill.*

17 Ramsden, *Man of the Century*, p. 508. Also see Peter Clarke, *The Last 1000 Days of the British Empire: Roosevelt, Churchill and the Birth of the Pax Americana* (London: Bloomsbury, 2009).

18 Martin Gilbert, *Churchill and America* (London: Free Press, 2005).

19 Toye, *Churchill's Empire*, p. 240.

20 Peter Clarke, *Mr Churchill's Profession: Statesman, Writer, Orator* (London: Bloomsbury, 2013).

21 See, for instance, Alfred J. Taylor, *Empire Building: Unity of the English Speaking Races of the World* (Hobart, Australia: The Mercury, 1913).

22 Clarke, *Mr Churchill's Profession.*

23 Boris Johnson, *The Churchill Factor: How One Man Made History* (London: Hodder & Stoughton, 2015).

24 Gilbert, *Churchill and America*, pp. 52, 102.

25 Ibid., p. 143.

26 Felix Klos, 'Boris Johnson's abuse of Churchill', *History Today*, 1 June 2017; www.historytoday.com/felix-klos/boris-johnsons-abuse-churchill. See also Klos, *Churchill on Europe: The Untold Story of Churchill's European Project* (London: I. B. Tauris, 2017).

27 Stephen Kinnock, 'Brexit and Churchill's "three majestic circles" ', *Demos Quarterly*, 9 May 2016; https://quarterly.demos.co.uk/article/issue-9/brexit-churchill-majestic-circles/.

28 Churchill, *Winston Churchill's 9 October 1948 Speech to the 69th Annual Conservative Party Conference published in the Report of the Proceedings* (London: National Union of Conservative and Unionist Associations, 1948).

29 See, for instance, Hugo Young, *This Blessed Plot: Britain and Europe from Churchill to Blair* (Basingstoke: Macmillan, 1999).

30 Ramsden, *Man of the Century*, p. 313.

31 Antoine Capet, 'Review of Felix Klos's *Churchill on Europe: The Untold Story of Churchill's European Project*', *Cercles*, www.cercles.com/review/r80/Klos.html. See also Capet (ed.),

Britain, France and the Entente Cordiale since 1904 (Basingstoke: Palgrave Macmillan, 2006).

32 Toye, *Churchill's Empire*, p. 290.

Chapter 3　A Parting of the Ways

1 ' "European policy": a cabinet memorandum by Mr Bevin on creation of a "third world power of consolidation of the West" ', 18 October 1949, cited in Benjamin Grob-Fitzgibbon, *Continental Drift: Britain and Europe from the End of Empire to the Rise of Euroscepticism* (Cambridge: Cambridge University Press, 2016), p. 116.

2 John Darwin, *The Empire Project: The Rise and Fall of the British World System* (Cambridge: Cambridge University Press, 2009), p. 539.

3 See Federico Romero, 'Interdependence and integration in American eyes: from the Marshall Plan to currency convertibility', in Alan S. Milward et al. (eds), *The Frontier of National Sovereignty: History and Theory 1945–1992* (London: Routledge, 1994), p. 156.

4 Alan S. Milward, *The United Kingdom and the European Community, Vol 1: The Rise and Fall of a National Strategy, 1945–1963* (London: Frank Cass, 2002), p. 3.

5 *Economic Aspects of European Unity*, memorandum prepared by the Economic Sub-Committee of the United Europe Movement, March 1948, cited in Grob-Fitzgibbon, *Continental Drift*, p. 100.

6 Leo Amery, *British Links with Europe*, address to the University of London, 26 November 1945, cited ibid., p. 35.

7 Leo Amery, 'European unity and world peace', *Sunday Times*, 27 October 1946, cited ibid., p. 46.

8 Ibid.

9 1951 Conservative Party general election manifesto, www.conservativemanifesto.com/1951/1951-conservative-manifesto.shtml.

10 Michael Foot, Richard Crossman and Ian Mikardo, *Keep Left* (London: New Statesman, 1947).

11 ' "European unity": a statement by the National Executive Committee of the Labour Party, May 1950', cited in Grob-Fitzgibbon, *Continental Drift*, p. 136.

12 Ronald Hyam, *Britain's Declining Empire: The Road to Decolonisation, 1918–1968* (Cambridge: Cambridge University Press, 2006), p. 214.

13 Darwin, *The Empire Project*.

14 James Belich, *Paradise Reforged: A History of the New Zealanders from the 1880s to the Year 2000* (London: Allen Lane, 2001), pp. 392–3.

15 Pearson, cited in in Hyam, *Britain's Declining Empire*, p. 310.

16 See John Lambert, ' "The last outpost": the Natalians, South Africa, and the British Empire', in Robert Bickers (ed.), *Settlers and Expatriates: Britons Over the Seas* (Oxford: Oxford University Press, 2010).

17 Alan S. Milward, *The European Rescue of the Nation-State* (London: Routledge 1992), p. 393.

18 Milward, *The United Kingdom and the European Community*, pp. 271–2.

19 Hansard, HC Deb 02 August 1961, vol. 645: cc1480–606.

20 Philip Ziegler, *Edward Heath* (London: Harper Press, 2010), p. 118.

21 Hugo Young, *This Blessed Plot: Britain and Europe from Churchill to Blair* (London: Macmillan, 1999), p. 126.

22 Ibid., p. 146.

23 Hugh Gaitskell, *The Challenge of Coexistence* (London: Methuen, 1957), p. 60.

24 Labour Party, *Britain and the Common Market: Texts of Speeches Made at the 1962 Labour Party Conference by the Rt Hon. Hugh Gaitskell MP and the Rt Hon. George Brown MP, together with the Policy Statement Accepted by Conference* (London: Labour Party, 1962), p. 12.

25 Alex May, 'Commonwealth or Europe? Macmillan's dilemma, 1961–63', in May (ed.), *Britain, the Commonwealth and Europe* (Basingstoke: Palgrave, 2001), p. 82.

26 Cited in Hyam, *Britain's Declining Empire*, p. 397.

27 These points are drawn from C. R. Schenk, 'Sterling, international monetary reform and Britain's applications to join the European Economic Community in the 1960s', *Contemporary European History*, 11/3 (2002), pp. 345–69.

28 Cited in Young, *This Blessed Plot*, p. 231.

29 Churchill Archives Centre, Julian Amery Papers, 1/10/16: Part 1, Letter from Julian Amery to Edward Heath, May 1974.

Chapter 4   The Powellite Interlude

1 For an in-depth discussion of Powell's significance for the national political outlook of the Conservative Party, see Andrew Gamble, *The Conservative Nation* (London: Routledge, 2011).

2 Chris Gifford, *The Making of Eurosceptic Britain: Identity and Economy in a Post-Imperial State* (Aldershot: Ashgate, 2008).

3 For an assessment of the early part of Powell's career, see especially Simon Heffer, *Like the Roman: The Life of Enoch Powell* (London: Faber & Faber, 2008), and T. E. Utley, *Enoch Powell: The Man and His Thinking* (London: HarperCollins, 1968).

4 Heffer, *Like the Roman*, p. 111.

5 See ibid., pp. 71, 74, 900–1.

6 These themes in his thinking are discussed in Gamble, *The Conservative Nation*, and Iain McLean, *Rational Choice and British Politics: An Analysis of Rhetoric and Manipulation from Peel to Blair* (Oxford: Oxford University Press, 2001), pp. 136–44.

7 See Roger Scruton, 'The language of Enoch Powell', in Lord Howard of Rising (ed.), *Enoch at 100: A Re-evaluation of the Life, Philosophy and Politics of Enoch Powell* (London: Biteback, 2014), pp. 114–22.

8 Ben Wellings, 'Enoch Powell: the lonesome leader', *Humanities Research*, 19/1 (2003), pp. 45–59.

9 Heffer, *Like the Roman*, p. 334.

10 Angus Maude and Enoch Powell, *Biography of a Nation: A Short History of Britain* (London: Pitman, 1955).

11 Powell, speech made to the Churchill Society, London, 23 April 1961, www.churchill-society-london.org.uk/StGeorg*.html.

12 See also Scruton, 'The language of Enoch Powell'.

13 For a detailed account of the lead up to this speech and the contexts shaping it, see Utley, *Enoch Powell*, pp. 13–44.

14 This is a quotation from Powell's 'Rivers of Blood' speech, delivered at a general meeting of the West Midlands Area Conservative Political Centre, 20 April 1968; see *The Telegraph*, 6 November 2007: www.telegraph.co.uk/

comment/3643823/Enoch-Powells-Rivers-of-Blood-speech.
html.

15 Peter Clarke, 'I am a classical scholar, and you are not',
London Review of Books, 35/5, 7 March 2013.

16 This issue is central to Paul Foot's *The Rise of Enoch Powell:
Examination of Enoch Powell's Attitude to Immigration and
Race* (London: Penguin, 1969). For a contrasting account,
see Heffer, *Like the Roman*.

17 Robert Pearce, 'Bad blood: Powell, Heath and the Tory
Party', *History Today*, 58/4 (2008), www.historytoday.com/
robert-pearce/bad-blood-powell-heath-and-tory-party.

18 This issue is explored in Heffer, *Like the Roman*.

19 These attributes are discussed in broader terms in Jan-Wer-
ner Müller, *What is Populism?* (Philadelphia: University of
Pennsylvania Press, 2016).

20 Geoffrey K. Fry, 'Parliament and "morality": Thatcher,
Powell, and populism', *Contemporary British History*, 12/1
(1998), pp. 139–47.

21 Fred Lindop, 'Racism and the working class: strikes in
support of Enoch Powell in 1968', *Labour History Review*,
66/1 (2001), pp. 79–99.

22 Amy Whipple, 'Revisiting the 'Rivers of Blood' controversy:
letters to Enoch Powell', *Journal of British Studies*, 48/3
(2009), pp. 717–35.

23 Ibid., p. 720.

24 Emma Vines, 'A common appeal: Anglo-British nationalism
and opposition to Europe, 1970–1975', *Australian Journal
of Politics and History*, 61/4 (2015), pp. 530–45.

25 Powell, speech at a press lunch, Brussels, 28 September
1972, in Richard Ritchie (ed.), *Enoch Powell: A Nation or
No Nation? Six Years in British Politics* (London: Batsford,
1978), p. 43.

26 Speech by the Rt Hon. J. Enoch Powell, MP, to a meeting
of the Belfast East Unionist Association, Kelly Hall, Belfast,
2 June 1972, http://enochpowell.info/Resources/June-Sept%
201972.pdf.

27 For a discussion of Powell's time in India, see Heffer, *Like
the Roman*, pp. 82–98.

28 See Roy Lewis, *Enoch Powell: Principle in Politics* (London:
Cassell, 1979).

29 Powell became a professor of Greek at the age of twenty-five at the University of Sydney. For an appreciation of the importance of classical sources upon his thinking, see Margaret Mountford, 'Enoch Powell as a classicist', in Howard, *Enoch at 100*.

30 Powell, 'Rivers of Blood' speech.

31 Camilla Schofield, *Enoch Powell and the Making of Postcolonial Britain* (Cambridge: Cambridge University Press, 2013).

32 Safraz Mansoor, 'Black Britain's darkest hour', *The Guardian*, 24 February 2008.

33 David Shiels, 'How Enoch Powell helped to shape modern Tory Euroscepticism', *LSE Brexit*, 3 June 2016, http://blogs.lse.ac.uk/brexit/2016/06/03/how-enoch-powell-helped-to-shape-modern-tory-euroscepticism/.

Chapter 5   The Anglosphere in the Late Twentieth Century

1 David Cannadine, *Margaret Thatcher: A Life and Legacy* (Oxford: Oxford University Press, 2017).

2 Stuart Hall, 'The great moving right show', *Marxism Today*, January 1979, http://banmarchive.org.uk/collections/mt/pdf/79_01_hall.pdf.

3 Anthony Barnett, *Iron Britannia: Why Parliament Waged its Falklands War* (London: Allison & Busby, 1992); and Ian Gilmore, 'Hauteur: review of Hugo Young's *The Blessed Plot*', *London Review of Books*, 10 December 1998, pp. 8–10.

4 David Sanders, Hugh Ward and David Marsh, 'Government popularity and the Falklands War: a reassessment', *British Journal of Political Science*, 17/3 (1987), pp. 281–313.

5 Philip Lynch, *The Politics of Nationhood: Sovereignty, Britishness and Conservative Politics* (Basingstoke: Palgrave, 1999).

6 Margaret Thatcher, 'Reason and religion: the moral foundations of freedom', James Bryce Lecture, 24 September 1996, www.margaretthatcher.org/document/108364.

7 Nicholas Wapshott, *Ronald Reagan and Margaret Thatcher: A Political Marriage* (London: Sentinel, 2008).

8 John Dumbrell, *A Special Relationship: Anglo-American Relations from the Cold War to Iraq* (Basingstoke: Palgrave, 2006).

9 Hugo Young, *This Blessed Plot: Britain and Europe from Churchill to Blair* (Basingstoke: Macmillan, 1999).

10 John Darwin, *The Empire Project: The Rise and Fall of the British World System* (Cambridge: Cambridge University Press, 2009).

11 Paul Sharp, *Thatcher's Diplomacy: The Revival of British Foreign Policy* (Basingstoke: Macmillan, 1997).

12 Ibid.

13 Cannadine, *Margaret Thatcher*, p. 34.

14 Young, *This Blessed Plot*.

15 Ibid.

16 Stephen George, *An Awkward Partner: Britain in the European Community* (Oxford: Oxford University Press, 2008).

17 Stephen Wall, *A Stranger in Europe: Britain and the EU from Thatcher to Blair* (Oxford: Oxford University Press, 2008).

18 Ibid.

19 Helen Thompson, *The British Conservative Government and the European Exchange Rate Mechanism* (London: Pinter, 1996).

20 Peter Katzenstein, 'United Germany in an integrating Europe', *Current History*, 96 (1997), pp. 116–23.

21 Wall, *A Stranger in Europe*.

22 Thompson, *The British Conservative Government and the European Exchange Rate Mechanism*.

23 Richard G. Whitman, 'On Europe: Margaret Thatcher's lasting legacy', Chatham House, 9 April 2013, www.chathamhouse.org/media/comment/view/190655.

24 Young, *This Blessed Plot*.

25 Sharp, *Thatcher's Diplomacy*.

26 Margaret Thatcher, 'Market entry is "urgent" ', *Finchley times*, 13 August 1971, www.margaretthatcher.org/document/102136.

27 Richard Vinen, *Thatcher's Britain: The Politics and Social Upheaval of the Thatcher Era* (London: Simon & Schuster, 2010).

28 See, for instance, her speech 'The language of liberty', given at the English-Speaking Union, New York, 7 December 1999, www.margaretthatcher.org/document/108386.

29 For an overview of its activities and writings, see Helen Baxendale and Ben Wellings, 'Euroscepticism and the Anglosphere: tradition and dilemmas in contemporary English nationalism', *Journal of Common Market Studies*, 53 (2015), pp. 123–39.

30 John Lloyd, 'The Anglosphere project', *New Statesman*, 13 March 2000, www.newstatesman.com/node/193400.

31 Conrad Black, 'Britain's Atlantic option', *The National Interest*, spring 1999, http://nationalinterest.org/article/britains-atlantic-option-357.

32 Conrad Black, *Britain's Final Choice: Europe or America?* (London: Centre for Policy Studies, 1998).

33 Lloyd, 'The Anglosphere project'.

34 Manmohan Singh, 'Of Oxford, economics, empire and freedom', *The Hindu*, 10 July 2005.

35 Daniel Hannan, *How We Invented Freedom and Why it Matters* (London: Head of Zeus, 2013).

36 Madhav Das Nalapat, 'India & the Anglosphere', *New Criterion*, January 2011, www.newcriterion.com/issues/2011/1/india-the-anglosphere.

37 Niall Ferguson, *Empire: How Britain Made the Modern World* (London: Penguin, 2004).

38 Andrew Roberts, *A History of the English-Speaking Peoples since 1900* (London: Phoenix, 2007).

39 Marc Steyn, 'Dependence day', *New Criterion*, January 2011, www.newcriterion.com/articles.cfm/Dependence-Day-6753.

40 Robert Conquest, *Reflections on a Ravaged Century* (London: W. W. Norton, 2001), pp. 267–8.

41 Robert Conquest, *Dragons of Expectation: Reality and Delusion in the Course of History* (London: Duckworth 2006), pp. 221–31.

42 Ibid., p. 222.

43 Ibid., pp. 224–5.

44 Thatcher, 'The language of liberty'.

45 Ibid.

46 James C. Bennett, 'Networking nation-states: the coming info-national order', *The National Interest*, no. 74 (winter 2003–4), pp. 17–30.

47 James C. Bennett, *The Anglosphere Challenge: Why the English-Speaking Nations Will Lead the Way in the Twenty-First Century* (Lanham, MD: Rowman & Littlefield, 2007).

48 Ibid.
49 James C. Bennett, 'The emerging Anglosphere', *Orbis*, 46/1 (2002).
50 John O'Sullivan, 'A British-led Anglosphere in world politics', *The Telegraph*, 29 December 2007.
51 Hannan, *How We Invented Freedom and Why it Matters*.

Chapter 6   The Eurosceptic Anglosphere Emerges

1 Stefano Gulmanelli, 'John Howard and the "Anglospherist" reshaping of Australia', *Australian Journal of Political Science*, 49/4 (2014), pp. 581–95.
2 John Howard, 'The Anglosphere and the advance of freedom', lecture to the Heritage Foundation, 28 September 2010, www.heritage.org/report/the-anglosphere-and-the-advance-freedom.
3 Daniel Hannan, *How We Invented Freedom and Why it Matters* (London: Head of Zeus, 2013), pp. 278–80.
4 Stephen Harper, Address to the Canada–UK Chamber of Commerce, 14 July 2006, www.canada-uk.org/event/speeches.
5 Phillip Gould, *The Unfinished Revolution: How the Modernisers Saved the Labour Party* (London: Little, Brown, 1998).
6 Chris Pierson and Francis G. Castles, 'Australian antecedents of the Third Way', *Political Studies*, 50 (2002), pp. 683–702.
7 Commission on Social Justice/Institute for Public Policy Research, *Social Justice: Strategies for National Renewal* (London: Vintage, 1994).
8 Tim Legrand, 'Elite, exclusive and elusive: transgovernmental policy networks and iterative policy transfer in the Anglosphere', *Policy Studies*, 37/5 (2016), pp. 440–55.
9 Francis Fukuyama, *The End of History and the Last Man* (London: Penguin, 1992), p. xxiii.
10 Samuel P. Huntington, 'The West: unique, not universal', *Foreign Affairs*, 75 (1996), pp. 28–46.
11 Rick Fawn, 'Canada: outside the Anglo-American fold', in Rick Fawn and Raymond Hinnebusch (eds), *The Iraq War: Causes and Consequences* (London: Lynne Rienner, 2006).

12 Walter Russell Mead, *God and Gold: Britain, America, and the Making of the Modern World* (New York: Vintage, 2007).

13 Ibid., p. 314.

14 Ibid., p. 95.

15 Perry Anderson, 'American foreign policy and its thinkers', *New Left Review*, no. 83 (2013) p. 122 [special issue].

16 The UKIP Manifesto 2015, www.ukip.org/manifesto2015.

17 William Hague, 'Britain and Australia: making the most of global opportunity', John Howard Lecture, 17 January 2013, www.menziesrc.org/images/Latest_News/PDF/Britain_and_Australia__making_the_most_of_global_opportunity1.pdf.

18 Boris Johnson, 'The Aussies are just like us, so let's stop kicking them out', *The Telegraph*, 25 August 2013, www.telegraph.co.uk/news/politics/10265619/The-Aussies-are-just-like-us-so-lets-stop-kicking-them-out.html.

19 Boris Johnson, Speech at Bloomberg in response to the receipt of Dr Gerard Lyons's publication of 'The Europe report: a win–win situation', 6 August 2014, www.london.gov.uk/sites/default/files/gla_migrate_files_destination/bj-europe-speech.pdf.

20 Tony Abbott, Address to Queen's College, Oxford University, 14 December 2012, www.australiantimes.co.uk/tony-abbott-address-to-queens-college-oxford-university/.

21 See, for example, Owen Paterson, 'The Anglosphere, trade and international security', speech to the Margaret Thatcher Center for Freedom, the Heritage Foundation, Washington, DC, 25 March 2015, www.uk2020.org.uk/wp-content/uploads/2014/10/The-Anglosphere-Trade-and-International-Security-UK-2020-25.03.2015-FINAL.pdf.

22 Shashi Parulekar and Joel Kotkin, 'The state of the Anglosphere', *City Journal* (winter 2012), www.city-journal.org/html/state-anglosphere-13447.html.

23 Daniel Hannan, *Why America Must Not Follow Europe* (New York: Encounter Books, 2011).

Chapter 7   Brexit:
The Anglosphere Triumphant

1 Tim Shipman, *All Out War: The Full Story of How Brexit Sank Britain's Political Class* (London: William Collins, 2016).

2 Michael Gove, secretary of state for justice, *Statement on the EU Referendum* (20 February 2016), www.voteleavetake-control.org/statement_from_michael_gove_mp_secretary_of_state_for_justice_on_the_eu_referendum.html.

3 Ibid.

4 Ibid.

5 David Davis, 'Britain would be better off outside the EU – and here's why', *ConservativeHome*, 4 February 2016, www.conservativehome.com/platform/2016/02/david-davis-britain-would-be-better-off-out-of-the-eu-and-heres-why.html.

6 Dominic Cummings, *On the Referendum #21: Branching Histories of the 2016 Referendum and 'the Frogs before the Storm'* (9 January 2017), accessed at https://dominiccummings.wordpress.com/2017/01/09/on-the-referendum-21-branching-histories-of-the-2016-refer-endum-and-the-frogs-before-the-storm-2/.

7 'London mayor under fire for remark about "part-Kenyan" Barack Obama', *The Guardian*, 22 April 2016, accessed at www.theguardian.com/politics/2016/apr/22/boris-johnson-barack-obama-kenyan-eu-referendum.

8 Helen Baxendale and Ben Wellings, 'Anglosphere cooperation given a surprise boost after Brexit vote', *LSE Policy and Politics blog*, 26 July 2016, http://blogs.lse.ac.uk/brexit/2016/07/26/after-the-brexit-vote-a-formalised-anglo-sphere-alliance-remains-unlikely/.

9 David Abulafia, 'Britain: apart from or part of Europe', *History Today*, 11 May 2015, www.historytoday.com/david-abulafia/britain-apart-or-part-europe; and various authors, 'Fog in channel, historians isolated', *History Today*, 18 May 2015, www.historytoday.com/various-authors/fog-channel-historians-isolated.

10 Anthony Barnett, *The Lure of Greatness: England's Brexit and America's Trump* (London: Unbound, 2017).

11 John O'Sullivan, 'Joseph Chamberlain, Theresa May's new lodestar', *The Spectator*, 16 July 2016, www.spectator.co.uk/2016/07/the-man-theresa-may-wants-to-be/.

12 Alan S. Milward, *The United Kingdom and the European Community*, Vol 1: *The Rise and Fall of a National Strategy, 1945–1963* (London: Frank Cass, 2002), p. 4.

13 Lee Rotherham, 'What would WTO mean? It would be a walk to a beach, not a cliff-edge drop to destruction', *ConservativeHome*, 22 May 2017, www.conservativehome.com/platform/2017/05/what-would-wto-mean-1-lee-rotherham-it-would-be-a-journey-to-prosperity-not-a-cliff-edge-drop-to-destruction.html.

14 Boris Johnson, 'Britain is back east of Suez', speech given in Bahrain, 9 December 2016, www.gov.uk/government/speeches/foreign-secretary-speech-britain-is-back-east-of-suez.

15 Valentina Romei, 'Twisting numbers and telling stories: Brexit and the Commonwealth', *Financial Times*, 28 April 2017, www.ft.com/content/2324edd8-2426-11e7-8691-d5f7e0cd0a16.

16 John Ravenhill, cited in Martin Kettle, 'Here is Britain's new place in the world – on the sidelines', *The Guardian*, 6 July 2017, www.theguardian.com/commentisfree/2017/jul/06/britain-world-sidelines-brexit-trump-theresa-may-g20.

17 Victor Hill, 'The Anglosphere is an emerging civilization-state', *MasterInvestor*, 8 June 2016, https://masterinvestor.co.uk/economics/anglosphere-emerging-civilization-state/.

18 James P. Pinkerton, 'Winning the war against Islamocommunism: we need a world anti-theocracy organization (WATO)', *Breitbart*, 15 June 2016, www.breitbart.com/national-security/2016/06/15/winning-war-islamocommunism/.

19 Chris Tomlinson, 'Kassam: Britain would have the "best relationship with the White House" if Farage was UK ambassador', *Breitbart*, 22 November 2016, www.breitbart.com/london/2016/11/22/kassam-theresa-may-wants-britain-powerful-diplomat-world-shed-make-farage-u-s-ambassador/.

20 Andrew Roberts, 'CANZUK: after Brexit, Canada, Australia, New Zealand and Britain can unite as a pillar of Western civilisation', *The Telegraph*, 13 September 2016, www.telegraph.co.uk/news/2016/09/13/canzuk-after-brexit-canada-australia-new-zealand-and-britain-can/.

21 James C. Bennett, 'Brexit boosts "CANZUK" replacement for European Union', *USA Today*, 24 June 2016, www.usatoday.com/story/opinion/columnist/2016/06/24/brexit-boosts-canzuk-replacement-european-union-column/86347818/.

22 Andrew Lilico, 'Which friends does Britain want?', *ConservativeHome*, 14 April 2014, www.conservativehome.com/

platform/2014/04/andrew-lilico-which-friends-does-britain-want.html.

23 Hill, 'The Anglosphere is an emerging civilization-state'.

24 James Paterson, 'Back of the queue? No, Britain's Commonwealth friends and allies will welcome Brexit', *City AM*, 28 June 2016, www.cityam.com/241014/back-of-the-queue-no-britains-commonwealth-friends-and-allies-would-welcome-brexit.

Conclusion

1 Patrick Joyce, *The State of Freedom: A Social History of the British State since 1800* (Cambridge: Cambridge University Press, 2013).

2 Peter Clarke, *The Locomotive of War: Money, Empire, Power and Guilt* (London: Bloomsbury Press, 2017).

3 John Hulsman, 'Theresa May can now play Elizabeth I in a new buccaneering age of Drake', *City AM*, 20 April 2017, www.cityam.com/263163/theresa-may-can-now-play-elizabeth-new-buccaneering-age.

4 Jon Wilson, *India Conquered* (London: Simon & Schuster, 2016).

5 Will Dahlgreen, 'The British Empire is something to be proud of', *YouGov*, 26 July 2014, https://yougov.co.uk/news/2014/07/26/britain-proud-its-empire/.

6 J. G. A. Pocock, 'History and sovereignty: the historiographical response to Europeanization in two British cultures', *Journal of British Studies*, 31/4 (1992), pp. 358–89.

7 Ibid., p. 373.

Index